Financial Theory with Python
A Gentle Introduction

Yves Hilpisch

Beijing · Boston · Farnham · Sebastopol · Tokyo

Financial Theory with Python

by Yves Hilpisch

Published by O'Reilly Media, Inc., 1005 Gravenstein Highway North, Sebastopol, CA 95472.

O'Reilly books may be purchased for educational, business, or sales promotional use. Online editions are also available for most titles (*http://oreilly.com*). For more information, contact our corporate/institutional sales department: 800-998-9938 or *corporate@oreilly.com*.

Acquisitions Editor: Michelle Smith	**Indexer:** nSight, Inc.
Development Editor: Michele Cronin	**Interior Designer:** David Futato
Production Editor: Daniel Elfanbaum	**Cover Designer:** Karen Montgomery
Copyeditor: Piper Editorial Conulting, LLC	**Illustrator:** Kate Dullea
Proofreader: Kim Cofer	

October 2021:   First Edition

Revision History for the First Edition
2021-09-23:   First Release

See *http://oreilly.com/catalog/errata.csp?isbn=9781098104351* for release details.

978-1-098-10435-1

[LSI]

Table of Contents

Preface

Python was quickly becoming the de-facto language for data science, machine learning and natural language processing; it would unlock new sources of innovation. Python would allow us to engage with its sizeable open source community, bringing state-of-the-art technology in-house quickly, while allowing for customization.[1]

—Kindman and Taylor (2021)

Why This Book?

Technological trends like online trading platforms, open source software, and open financial data have significantly lowered or even completely removed the barriers of entry to the global financial markets. Individuals with only limited amounts of cash at their free disposal can get started, for example, with algorithmic trading within hours. Students and academics in financial disciplines with a little bit of background knowledge in programming can easily apply cutting-edge innovations in machine and deep learning to financial data—on the notebooks they bring to their finance classes. On the hardware side, cloud providers offer professional compute and data processing capabilities starting at 5 USD per month, billed by the hour and with almost unlimited scalability. So far, academic and professional finance education has only partly reacted to these trends.

This book teaches both finance and the Python (*http://python.org*) programming language from the ground up. Nowadays, finance and programming in general are closely intertwined disciplines, with Python being one of the most widely used programming languages in the financial industry. The book presents relevant foundations—from mathematics, finance, and programming—in an integrated but not-too-technical fashion. Traditionally, theoretical finance and computational finance have been more or less separate disciplines. The fact that programming classes (for

---

[1] Kindman, Andrew and Tom Taylor, "Why We Rewrote Our USD30 Billion Asset Management Platform in Python." (March 29, 2021), *https://oreil.ly/GghS6.*

example, in Python but also in C++) have become an integral part of Master of Financial Engineering and similar university programs shows how important programming skills have become in the field.

However, *mathematical foundations*, *theoretical finance*, and *basic programming techniques* are still quite often taught independently from one another and only later in combination with *computational finance*. This book takes a different approach in that the mathematical concepts—for example, from linear algebra and probability theory—provide the common background against which financial ideas and programming techniques alike are introduced. Abstract mathematical concepts are thereby motivated from two different angles: finance and programming. In addition, this approach allows for a new learning experience since both mathematical and financial concepts can directly be translated into executable code that can then be explored interactively.

Several readers of one of my other books, *Python for Finance* (2nd ed., 2018, O'Reilly), pointed out that it teaches neither finance nor Python from the ground up. Indeed, the reader of that book is expected to have at least some experience in both finance *and* (Python) programming. *Financial Theory with Python* closes this gap in that it focuses on more fundamental concepts from both finance and Python programming. In that sense, readers who finish this book can naturally progress to *Python for Finance* to further build and improve their Python skills as applied to finance. More guidance is provided in the final chapter.

Target Audience

I have written a number of books about Python applied to finance. My company, The Python Quants, offers a number of live and online training classes in Python for finance. For all of my previous books and the training classes, the book readers and training participants are expected to already have some background knowledge in both finance and Python programming or a similar language.

This book starts completely from scratch, with just the expectation that the reader has some basic knowledge in mathematics, in particular from calculus, linear algebra, and probability theory. Although the book material is almost self-contained with regard to the mathematical concepts introduced, an introductory mathematics book like the one by Pemberton and Rau (2016)[2] is recommended for further details if needed.

Given this approach, this book targets students, academics, and professionals alike who want to learn about financial theory, financial data modeling, and the use of Python for computational finance. It is a systematic introduction to the field on which to build through more advanced books or training programs. Readers with a

---

2 Find the full reference for this title in Chapter 7.

formal financial background will find the mathematical and financial elements of the book rather simple and straightforward. On the other hand, readers with a stronger programming background will find the Python elements rather simple and easy to understand.

Even if the reader does not intend to move on to more advanced topics in computational finance, algorithmic trading, or asset management, the Python and finance skills acquired through this book can be applied beneficially to standard problems in finance, such as the composition of investment portfolios according to modern portfolio theory (MPT). This book also teaches, for example, how to value options and other derivatives by standard methods such as replication portfolios or risk-neutral pricing.

This book is also suitable for executives in the financial industry who want to learn about the Python programming language as applied to finance. On the other hand, it can also be read by those already proficient in Python or another programming language who want to learn more about the application of Python in finance.

Overview of the Book

The book consists of the following chapters:

Chapter 1
> The first chapter sets the stage for the rest of the book. It provides a concise history of finance, explains the book's approach to using Python for finance, and shows how to set up a basic Python infrastructure suited to work with the code provided and the Jupyter Notebooks that accompany the book.

Chapter 2
> This chapter covers the most simple model economy, in which the analysis of finance under uncertainty is possible: there are only two relevant dates and two uncertain future states possible. One sometimes speaks of a *static two-state economy*. Despite its simplicity, the framework allows the introduction of such basic notions of finance as net present value, expected return, volatility, contingent claims, option replication, arbitrage pricing, martingale measures, market completeness, risk-neutral pricing, and mean-variance portfolios.

Chapter 3
> This chapter introduces a third uncertain future state to the model, analyzing a *static three-state economy*. This allows us to analyze such notions as market incompleteness, indeterminacy of martingale measures, super-replication of contingent claims, and approximate replication of contingent claims. It also introduces the Capital Asset Pricing Model as an equilibrium pricing approach for financial assets.

Chapter 4

In this chapter, agents with their individual decision problems are introduced. The analysis in this chapter mainly rests on the dominating paradigm in finance for decision making under uncertainty: *expected utility maximization*. Based on a so-called representative agent, equilibrium notions are introduced, and the connection between optimality and equilibrium on the one hand and martingale measures and risk-neutral pricing on the other hand are illustrated. The representative agent is also one way of overcoming the difficulties that arise in economies with incomplete markets.

Chapter 5

This chapter generalizes the previous notions and results in a setting with a finite, but possibly large, number of uncertain future states. It requires a bit more mathematical formalism to analyze this *general static economy*.

Chapter 6

Building on the analysis of the general static economy, this chapter introduces dynamics to the financial modeling arsenal—to analyze two special cases of a dynamic economy in discrete time. The basic insight is that uncertainty about future states of an economy in general resolves gradually over time. This can be modeled by the use of stochastic processes, an example of which is the binomial process that can be represented visually by a binomial tree.

Chapter 7

The final chapter provides a wealth of additional resources to explore in the fields of mathematics, financial theory, and Python programming. It also provides guidance on how to proceed after the reader has finished this book.

Conventions Used in This Book

The following typographical conventions are used in this book:

Italic

Indicates new terms, URLs, email addresses, filenames, and file extensions.

`Constant width`

Used for program listings, as well as within paragraphs to refer to program elements such as variable or function names, databases, data types, environment variables, statements, and keywords.

Constant width bold

Shows commands or other text that should be typed literally by the user.

Constant width italic

Shows text that should be replaced with user-supplied values or with values determined by context.

This element signifies a general note.

This element indicates a warning or caution.

This element indicates important information.

Using Code Examples

Supplemental material (code examples, exercises, etc.) is available for download at *https://finpy.pqp.io*.

If you have a technical question or a problem using the code examples, please send email to *bookquestions@oreilly.com*.

This book is here to help you get your job done. In general, if example code is offered with this book, you may use it in your programs and documentation. You do not need to contact us for permission unless you're reproducing a significant portion of the code. For example, writing a program that uses several chunks of code from this book does not require permission. Selling or distributing examples from O'Reilly books does require permission. Answering a question by citing this book and quoting example code does not require permission. Incorporating a significant amount of example code from this book into your product's documentation does require permission.

We appreciate, but generally do not require, attribution. An attribution usually includes the title, author, publisher, and ISBN. For example, this book would be attributed as *"Financial Theory with Python* by Yves Hilpisch (O'Reilly). Copyright 2022 Yves Hilpisch, 978-1-098-10435-1."

If you feel your use of code examples falls outside fair use or the permission given above, feel free to contact us at *permissions@oreilly.com*.

O'Reilly Online Learning

 For more than 40 years, *O'Reilly Media* has provided technology and business training, knowledge, and insight to help companies succeed.

Our unique network of experts and innovators share their knowledge and expertise through books, articles, and our online learning platform. O'Reilly's online learning platform gives you on-demand access to live training courses, in-depth learning paths, interactive coding environments, and a vast collection of text and video from O'Reilly and 200+ other publishers. For more information, visit *http://oreilly.com*.

How to Contact Us

Please address comments and questions concerning this book to the publisher:

O'Reilly Media, Inc.
1005 Gravenstein Highway North
Sebastopol, CA 95472
800-998-9938 (in the United States or Canada)
707-829-0515 (international or local)
707-829-0104 (fax)

We have a web page for this book, where we list errata, examples, and any additional information. You can access this page at *https://oreil.ly/fin-theory-with-python*.

Email *bookquestions@oreilly.com* to comment or ask technical questions about this book.

For news and information about our books and courses, visit *http://oreilly.com*.

Find us on Facebook: *http://facebook.com/oreilly*.

Follow us on Twitter: *http://twitter.com/oreillymedia*.

Watch us on YouTube: *http://www.youtube.com/oreillymedia*.

Acknowledgments

This book has benefited from valuable feedback by delegates of our Certificate Programs in Python for Finance. They have pointed out numerous improvements over time.

I am thankful for several helpful comments that I have received from the technical reviewers.

I am also grateful for the help and support that I have experienced from the whole O'Reilly team.

I dedicate this book to my wife Sandra. You are the love of my life.

## CHAPTER 1

Finance and Python

The history of finance theory is an interesting example of the interaction between abstract theorizing and practical application.

—Frank Milne (1995)

Hedge funds have sucked in tens of billions of dollars in investments in recent years, assisted increasingly by technology. The same tech is also benefiting those people who make the financial decisions at these organisations.

—Laurence Fletcher (2020)

This chapter gives a concise overview of topics relevant for the book. It is intended to provide both the financial and technological framework for the chapters to follow. "A Brief History of Finance" on page 2 starts by giving a brief overview of the history and current state of finance. "Major Trends in Finance" on page 3 discusses the major trends that have been driving the evolution of finance over time: mathematics, technology, data, and artificial intelligence. Against this background, "A Four-Languages World" on page 4 argues that finance today is a discipline of four closely interconnected types of languages: English, finance, mathematics, and programming. The overall approach of the book is explained in "The Approach of This Book" on page 5. "Getting Started with Python" on page 8 illustrates how an appropriate Python environment can be installed on the reader's computer. However, all the code can be used and executed via a regular web browser on the Quant Platform (*http://finpy.pqp.io*) so that a local Python installation can be set up later.

A Brief History of Finance

To better understand the current state of finance and the financial industry, it is help-ful to have a look at how they have developed over time. The history of finance as a scientific field can be divided roughly into three periods according to Rubinstein (2006):

The ancient period (pre-1950)
: A period mainly characterized by informal reasoning, rules of thumb, and the experience of market practitioners.

The classical period (1950–1980)
: A period characterized by the introduction of formal reasoning and mathematics to the field. Specialized models (for example, Black and Scholes's (1973) option pricing model) as well as general frameworks (for example, Harrison and Kreps's (1979) risk-neutral pricing approach) were developed during this period.

The modern period (1980–2000)
: This period generated many advances in specific subfields of finance (for exam-ple, computational finance) and tackled, among others, important empirical phe-nomena in the financial markets, such as stochastic interest rates (for example, Cox, Ingersoll, and Ross (1985)) or stochastic volatility (for example, Heston (1993)).

Fifteen years after the publication of the Rubinstein (2006) book, we can add fourth and fifth periods today. These two periods are responsible for the rise and the current omnipresence of Python in finance:

The computational period (2000–2020)
: This period saw a shift from a theoretical focus in finance to a computational one, driven by advances in both hardware and software used in finance. The paper by Longstaff and Schwartz (2001)—providing an efficient numerical algo-rithm to value American options by Monte Carlo simulation—illustrates this paradigm shift quite well. Their algorithm is computationally demanding in that hundreds of thousands of simulations and multiple ordinary least-squares regres-sions are required in general to value only a single option (see Hilpisch (2018)).

The artificial intelligence period (post-2020)
: Advances in artificial intelligence (AI) and related success stories have spurred interest to make use of the capabilities of AI in the financial domain. While there are already successful applications of AI in finance (see Hilpisch (2020)), it can be assumed that from 2020 onward there will be a systematic paradigm shift toward *AI-first finance*. AI-first finance describes the shift from simple, in general linear, models in finance to the use of advanced models and algorithms from AI

—such as deep neural networks or reinforcement learning—to capture, describe, and explain financial phenomena.

Major Trends in Finance

Like many other subjects and industries, finance has become a more formalized scientific discipline over time, driven by the increasing use of formal mathematics, advanced technology, increasing data availability, and improved algorithms, such as those from AI. Taken together, the evolution of finance over time can therefore be characterized by four major trends:

Mathematics

Starting in the 1950s with the classical period, finance has become a more and more formalized discipline, making systematic use of different fields in mathematics, like linear algebra or stochastic calculus. The mean-variance portfolio (MVP) theory by Markowitz (1952) can be considered a major breakthrough in quantitative finance if not its starting point itself—leaving the ancient period characterized mainly by informal reasoning behind.

Technology

The widespread availability and use of personal computers, workstations, and servers, starting mainly in the late 1980s and early 1990s, brought more and more technology to the field. While compute power and capacity in the beginning were rather limited, they have reached levels as of today that allow us to attack even the most complex problems in finance by sheer brute force, often rendering the search for rather specialized, efficient models and methods—that characterized the classical and modern periods—obsolete. The credo has become "Scale your hardware and use modern software in combination with appropriate numerical methods." On the other hand, the modern hardware found in most dorm and living rooms is already powerful enough that even high-performance approaches, like parallel processing, can generally be used on such commodity hardware—lowering the barriers of entry to computational and AI-first finance tremendously.

Data

While researchers and practitioners alike mainly relied on printed financial information and data in the ancient and classical periods (think of the *Wall Street Journal* or the *Financial Times*), electronic financial data sets have become more widely available starting in the modern period. However, the computational period has seen an explosion in the availability of financial data. High-frequency intraday data sets have become the norm and have replaced end-of-day closing prices as the major basis for empirical research. A single stock might generate intraday data sets with well over 100,000 data points every trading day—this number is roughly the equivalent of 400 years' worth of end-of-day closing prices for the same stock (250 trading days per year times 400 years). Even more recently, a proliferation in open or free data sets has been observed, which also significantly lowers the barriers of entry to computational finance, algorithmic trading, or financial econometrics.

Artificial intelligence
The availability of ever more financial data ("big financial data") makes the application of AI algorithms—such as those from machine learning, deep learning, or reinforcement learning (see Hilpisch (2020))—not only possible but also in many cases these days necessary. Traditional statistical methods from financial econometrics are often not suited anymore to cope with today's complexities in financial markets. Faced with nonlinear, multidimensional, ever-changing financial environments, AI-based algorithms might often be the only option to discover relevant relationships and patterns, generate valuable insights, and benefit from improved prediction capabilities.

By reading this book, the reader lays the foundations in the areas of financial mathematics and modern technology used to implement formal financial models. The reader also acquires skills to work with typical financial data sets encountered in finance. Taken together, this prepares the reader to later on also explore more easily advanced topics in computational finance or AI as applied to finance.

Python and Finance

More and more, finance has become a field driven by computationally demanding algorithms, ever-increasing data availability, and AI. Python has proven to be the right programming language and technology platform to address the requirements and challenges that arise from the major trends observed in the field.

A Four-Languages World

Against this background, finance has become a world of four languages:

Natural language
Today, the *English* language is the only relevant language in the field when it comes to published research, books, articles, or news.

Financial language
Like every other field, *finance* has technical terms, notions, and expressions that describe certain phenomena or ideas that are usually not relevant in other domains.

Mathematical language

  Mathematics is the tool and language of choice when it comes to formalizing the notions and concepts of finance.

Programming language

  As the quote at the beginning of the preface points out, *Python* (*http:// python.org*) as a programming language has become the language of choice in many corners of the financial industry.

The mastery of finance therefore requires both the academic and practitioner to be fluent in all four languages: English, finance, mathematics, and Python. This is *not* to say that, for instance, English and Python are the *only* relevant natural or programming languages. It is rather the case that if you have only a limited amount of time to learn a programming language, you should most probably focus on Python—alongside mathematical finance—on your way to mastery of the field.

The Approach of This Book

How does this book approach the four languages needed in finance? The English language is a no-brainer—you are reading it already. Yet, three remain.

For example, this book cannot introduce every single piece of mathematics in detail that is needed in finance. Nor can it introduce every single concept in (Python) programming in detail that is needed in computational finance. However, it tries to introduce related concepts from finance, mathematics, and programming alongside one another whenever possible and sensible.

From Chapter 2 onward, the book introduces a financial notion or concept and then illustrates it on the basis of both a mathematical representation and the implementation in Python. As an example, have a look at the following table from Chapter 3. The table lists the financial topic, the major mathematical elements, and the major Python data structure used to implement the financial mathematics:

Finance	Mathematics	Python
Uncertainty	Probability space	ndarray
Financial assets	Vectors, matrices	ndarray
Attainable contingent claims	Span of vectors, basis of vector space	ndarray

The following is a walkthrough of one specific example, details of which are provided in later chapters. The example is only for illustration of the general approach of the book at this point.

As an example, take the central concept of *uncertainty* in finance from the preceding table. Uncertainty embodies the notion that future states of a model economy are not known in advance. Which future state of the economy unfolds might be important, for example, to determine the payoff of a European call option. In a discrete case, one deals with a finite number of such states, like two, three, or more. In the most simple case of two future states only, the payoff of a European call option is represented mathematically as a *random variable*, which in turn can be represented formally as a *vector v* that is itself an element of the *vector space* $\mathbb{R}^2$. A vector space is a collection of objects—called vectors—for which addition and scalar multiplication are defined. Formally, one writes for such a vector *v*, for example:

$$v = \begin{pmatrix} v^u \\ v^d \end{pmatrix} \in \mathbb{R}^2_{\geq 0}$$

Here, both elements of the vector are assumed to be non-negative real numbers $v^u, v^d \in \mathbb{R}_{\geq 0}$. More concretely, if the uncertain, state-dependent price of the stock on which the European call option is written is given in this context by

$$S = \begin{pmatrix} 20 \\ 5 \end{pmatrix} \in \mathbb{R}^2_{\geq 0}$$

and the strike price of the option is $K = 15$, the payoff C of the European call option is given by

$$C = \max(S - K, 0) = \begin{pmatrix} \max(20 - 15, 0) \\ \max(5 - 15, 0) \end{pmatrix} = \begin{pmatrix} 5 \\ 0 \end{pmatrix} \in \mathbb{R}^2_{\geq 0}$$

This illustrates how the notions of the *uncertain price of a stock* and the *state-dependent payoff of a European option* can be modeled mathematically as a vector. The discipline dealing with vectors and vector spaces in mathematics is called *linear algebra*.

How can all this be translated into Python programming? First, *real numbers* are represented as *floating point numbers* or `float` objects in Python:

```
In [1]: vu = 1.5   ❶

In [2]: vd = 3.75  ❷

In [3]: type(vu)   ❸
Out[3]: float

In [4]: vu + vd    ❹
Out[4]: 5.25
```

❶ Defines a variable with the name vu and the value 1.5.

❷ Defines a variable with the name vd and the value 3.75.

❸ Looks up the type of the vu object—it is a `float` object.

❹ Adds up the values of vu and vd.

Second, one usually calls collections of objects of the same type in programming *arrays*. In Python, the package NumPy (*http://numpy.org*) provides support for such data structures. The major data structure provided by this package is called `ndarray`, which is an abbreviation for *n*-dimensional array. Real-valued vectors are straightforward to model with NumPy:

```
In [5]: import numpy as np   ❶

In [6]: v = np.array((vu, vd))   ❷

In [7]: v   ❸
Out[7]: array([1.5 , 3.75])

In [8]: v.dtype   ❹
Out[8]: dtype('float64')

In [9]: v.shape   ❺
Out[9]: (2,)

In [10]: v + v   ❻
Out[10]: array([3. , 7.5])

In [11]: 3 * v   ❼
Out[11]: array([ 4.5 , 11.25])
```

❶ Imports the NumPy package.

❷ Instantiates an `ndarray` object.

❸ Prints out the data stored in the object.

❹ Looks up the data type for all elements.

❺ Looks up the shape of the object.

❻ Vector addition illustrated.

❼ Scalar multiplication illustrated.

This shows how the mathematical concepts surrounding vectors are represented and applied in Python. It is then only one step further to apply those insights to finance:

```
In [12]: S = np.array((20, 5))   ❶

In [13]: K = 15   ❷

In [14]: C = np.maximum(S - K, 0)   ❸

In [15]: C   ❹
Out[15]: array([5, 0])
```

❶ Defines the uncertain price of the stock as an `ndarray` object.

❷ Defines the strike price as a Python variable with an integer value (`int` object).

❸ Calculates the maximum expression element-wise.

❹ Shows the resulting data now stored in the `ndarray` object `C`.

This illustrates the style and approach of this book:

1. Notions and concepts in finance are introduced.

2. A mathematical representation and model is provided.

3. The mathematical model is translated into executable Python code.

In that sense, finance motivates the use of mathematics, which in turn motivates the use of Python programming techniques.

Getting Started with Python

One of the benefits of Python is that it is an open source language, which holds true for the absolute majority of important packages as well. This allows for easy installation of the language and required packages on all major operating systems, such as macOS, Windows, and Linux. There are only a few major packages that are required for the code of this book and finance in general in addition to a basic Python interpreter:

NumPy (*http://numpy.org*)
: This package allows the efficient handling of large, n-dimensional numerical data sets.

pandas (*http://pandas.pydata.org*)
: This package is primarily for the efficient handling of tabular data sets, such as financial time series data. Although not required for the purposes of this book, pandas has become one of the most popular Python packages in finance.

SciPy *(http://scipy.org)*

This package is a collection of scientific functions that are required, for example, to solve typical optimization problems.

SymPy *(http://sympy.org)*

This package allows for symbolic mathematics with Python, which sometimes comes in handy when dealing with financial models and algorithms.

`matplotlib` *(http://matplotlib.org)*

This package is the standard package in Python for visualization. It allows you to generate and customize different types of plots, such as line plots, bar charts, and histograms.

Similarly, there are only two tools that are required to get started with interactive Python coding:

IPython (http://ipython.org)

This is the most popular environment in which to do interactive Python coding on the command line (terminal, shell).

JupyterLab (http://jupyter.org)

This is the interactive development environment in which to do interactive Python coding and development in the browser.

The technical prerequisites to follow along with regard to Python programming are minimal. There are basically two options for making use of the Python code in this book:

Quant Platform

On the Quant Platform (*http://finpy.pqp.io*), for which you can sign up for free, you find a full-fledged environment for interactive financial analytics with Python. This allows you to make use of the Python code provided in this book via the browser, making a local installation unnecessary. After signing up for free, you have automatic access to all code and all Jupyter Notebooks that accompany the book, and you can execute the code right away in the browser.

Local Python environment

It is also straightforward nowadays to install a local Python environment that allows you to dive into financial analytics and the book code on your own computer. This section describes how to do this.

Local Installation Versus the Quant Platform

From experience, the local installation of an appropriate Python environment can sometimes prove difficult for someone who is just starting out in the programming world. Therefore, it is recommended that you do not spend too much time at the beginning on installing Python locally if you face any issues. Rather, make use of the Quant Platform (*http://finpy.pqp.io*) and later on, with some more experience, you can still return and install Python on your local machine.

An easy and modern way of installing Python is by the use of the conda (*http://conda.io*) package and environment manager (see Figure 1-1).

Figure 1-1. conda web page

The most efficient way to install conda and a basic Python interpreter is via the Miniconda (*https://oreil.ly/NI0Wi*) distribution. On the Miniconda download page (*https://oreil.ly/gaWTP*), installer packages for the most important operating systems and Python versions are provided (see Figure 1-2). Additional options, such as for Apple's M1 chips ("Apple Silicon"), are provided by the Miniforge project (*https://oreil.ly/gKeo3*).

Figure 1-2. Miniconda download page

After having installed Miniconda or Miniforge according to the guidelines provided for your operating system, you should open a shell or command prompt and check whether conda is available. The examples that follow are based on conda as installed via Miniforge on an Apple Mac computer with the M1 chip. You should get an output similar to this:

```
(base) minione:finpy yves$ conda --version
conda 4.10.3
(base) minione:finpy yves$
```

Also note the (base) part of the prompt that is typical for conda-based Python installations. The next step is to create a new *Python environment* as follows (and to answer "y" when prompted):

```
pro:finpy yves$ conda create --name finpy python=3.9
...
Preparing transaction: done
Verifying transaction: done
Executing transaction: done
#
# To activate this environment, use
#
#     $ conda activate finpy
#
# To deactivate an active environment, use
#
#     $ conda deactivate
```

After the successful completion, activate the environment as follows:

```
(base) minione:finpy yves$ conda activate finpy
(finpy) minione:finpy yves$
```

Notice how the prompt changes. Next, install the required tools IPython and Jupyter-Lab as follows (and answer "y" when prompted):

```
(finpy) minione:finpy yves$ conda install ipython jupyterlab
...
```

After that, you should install the major Python packages generally used for financial data science as follows (the flag -y avoids the confirmation prompt):

```
(finpy) minione:finpy yves$ conda install -y numpy pandas matplotlib scipy sympy
...
```

This provides the most important Python packages for data analysis in general and financial analytics in particular. You might check whether everything has been installed as follows:

```
(finpy) minione:finpy yves$ conda list
# packages in environment at /Users/yves/Python/envs/finpy:
#
# Name                    Version                   Build  Channel
anyio                     3.3.0            py39h2804cbe_0    conda-forge
appnope                   0.1.2            py39h2804cbe_1    conda-forge
argon2-cffi               20.1.0           py39h5161555_2    conda-forge
...
jupyterlab                3.1.12             pyhd8ed1ab_0    conda-forge
...
numpy                     1.21.2           py39h1f3b974_0    conda-forge
...
python                    3.9.7        h54d631c_1_cpython    conda-forge
...
zipp                      3.5.0              pyhd8ed1ab_0    conda-forge
zlib                      1.2.11             h31e879b_1009    conda-forge
zstd                      1.5.0              h861e0a7_0    conda-forge
(finpy) minione:finpy yves$
```

An interactive Python session is then started by simply typing python:

```
(finpy) minione:finpy yves$ python
Python 3.9.7 | packaged by conda-forge | (default, Sep 14 2021, 01:14:24)
[Clang 11.1.0 ] on darwin
Type "help", "copyright", "credits" or "license" for more information.
>>> print('Hello Finance World.')
Hello Finance World.
>>> exit()
(finpy) minione:finpy yves$
```

A better interactive shell is provided by IPython, which is started via `ipython` on the shell:

```
(finpy) minione:finpy yves$ ipython
Python 3.9.7 | packaged by conda-forge | (default, Sep 14 2021, 01:14:24)
Type 'copyright', 'credits' or 'license' for more information
IPython 7.27.0 -- An enhanced Interactive Python. Type '?' for help.

In [1]: from numpy.random import default_rng

In [2]: rng = default_rng(100)

In [3]: rng.random(10)
Out[3]:
array([0.83498163, 0.59655403, 0.28886324, 0.04295157, 0.9736544 ,
       0.5964717 , 0.79026316, 0.91033938, 0.68815445, 0.18999147])

In [4]: exit
(finpy) minione:finpy yves$
```

However, it is recommended—especially for the Python beginner—to work with JupyterLab in the browser. To this end, type `jupyter lab` on the shell, which should give an output with messages similar to the following:

```
(finpy) minione:finpy yves$ jupyter lab
...
[I 2021-09-16 14:18:21.774 ServerApp] Jupyter Server 1.11.0 is running at:
[I 2021-09-16 14:18:21.774 ServerApp] http://localhost:8888/lab
[I 2021-09-16 14:18:21.774 ServerApp]  or http://127.0.0.1:8888/lab
[I 2021-09-16 14:18:21.774 ServerApp] Use Control-C to stop this server
         and shut down all kernels (twice to skip confirmation).
```

In general, a new browser tab is opened automatically, which then shows you the starting page of JupyterLab similar to Figure 1-3.

You can then open a new Jupyter Notebook and start with interactive Python coding, as shown in Figure 1-4. To write code in a cell, click on the cell. To execute the code, use Shift-Return, Ctrl-Return, or Alt-Return (you will notice the difference).

Figure 1-3. JupyterLab start page

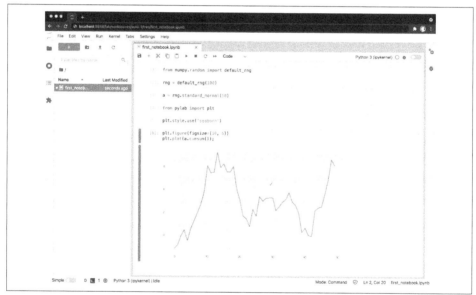

Figure 1-4. New Jupyter Notebook

You can also open one of the Jupyter Notebook files provided with this book (see Figure 1-5).

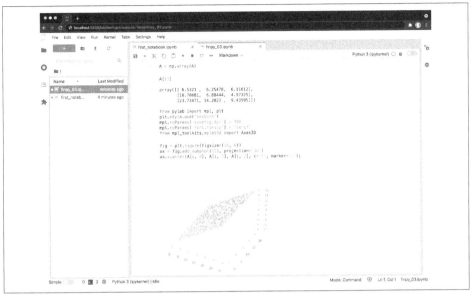

Figure 1-5. Jupyter Notebook accompanying the book

This section just provides the very basics to get started with Python and related tools, such as IPython and JupyterLab. For more details—for example, about how to work with IPython—refer to the book by VanderPlas (2016) listed in Chapter 7.

Conclusions

Finance can look back on a long history. The period from 1950 to 1980 is characterized by the introduction of rigorous mathematical analysis to the field. From the 1980s onward, and in particular since 2000, the role of computers and computational finance has gained tremendously in importance. This trend will be further reinforced by the increasing role AI plays in the field, with its computationally demanding algorithms from machine learning (ML) and deep learning (DL).

The finance field makes use of four different types of language: *natural language* (English in general), *financial language* (notions and expressions special to the field), *mathematical language* (like linear algebra or probability theory), and *programming language* (like Python for the purposes of this book).

The approach of this book is to introduce related concepts from finance, mathematics, and Python programming alongside one another. The necessary prerequisites on the Python side are minimal, with the conda package and environment manager often as the tool of choice nowadays to manage Python environments.

You are now ready to move on to Chapter 2, which discusses the most simple financial model presented in the book and introduces many of the central finance notions. The intuition that you gain in the most simple financial model should easily carry over to the more advanced models and approaches discussed from Chapter 3 onward.

References

Articles and books cited in this chapter:

Cox, John, Jonathan Ingersoll and Stephen Ross. 1985. "A Theory of the Term Structure of Interest Rates." *Econometrica* 53 (2): 385–407.

Fletcher, Laurence. 2020. "Hedge Funds Exploit Technology to Reduce Cost and Waste." *Financial Times*, December 15, 2020. *https://oreil.ly/HE4Cc*.

Heston, Steven. 1993. "A Closed-Form Solution for Options with Stochastic Volatility with Applications to Bond and Currency Options." *The Review of Financial Studies* 6 (2): 327–343.

Hilpisch, Yves. 2018. *Python for Finance: Mastering Data-Driven Finance*. 2nd ed. Sebastopol: O'Reilly.

Hilpisch, Yves. 2020. *Artificial Intelligence in Finance: A Python-Based Guide*. Sebastopol: O'Reilly.

Longstaff, Francis and Eduardo Schwartz. 2001. "Valuing American Options by Simulation: A Simple Least Squares Approach." *Review of Financial Studies* 14 (1): 113–147.

Markowitz, Harry. 1952. "Portfolio Selection." *Journal of Finance* 7 (1): 77-91.

Milne, Frank. 1995. *Finance Theory and Asset Pricing*. New York: Oxford University Press.

Rubinstein, Mark. 2006. *A History of the Theory of Investments*. Hoboken: Wiley Finance.

Two-State Economy

As an empirical domain, finance is aimed at specific answers, such as an appropriate value for a given security, or an optimal number of its shares to hold.

 —Darrell Duffie (1988)

The notion of arbitrage is crucial to the modern theory of Finance.

 —Delbaen and Schachermayer (2006)

The analysis in this chapter is based on the most simple *model economy* that is still rich enough to introduce many important notions and concepts of finance: an economy with two relevant points in time and two uncertain future states only. It also allows us to present some important results in the field, like the *Fundamental Theorems of Asset Pricing*, that are discussed in this chapter.[1]

The simple model chosen is a means to simplify the formal introduction of the sometimes rather abstract mathematical concepts and financial ideas by avoiding as many technicalities as possible. Once these ideas are fleshed out and well understood, the transfer to more realistic financial models usually proves seamless.

This chapter covers mainly the following central topics from finance, mathematics, and Python programming:

Finance	Mathematics	Python
Time	Natural numbers $\mathbb{N}$	int, type
Money (currency)	Real numbers $\mathbb{R}$	float
Cash flow	Tuple	tuple, list

---

1 For details on the Fundamental Theorems of Asset Pricing, refer to the seminal papers by Harrison and Kreps (1979) and Harrison and Pliska (1981).

Finance	Mathematics	Python
Return, interest	Real numbers $\mathbb{R}$	abs
(Net) present value	Function	def, return
Uncertainty	Vector space $\mathbb{R}^2$	NumPy, ndarray, np.array
Financial asset	Process	ndarray, tuple
Risk	Probability, state space, power set, mapping	ndarray
Expectation, expected return	Dot product	np.dot
Volatility	Variance, standard deviation	np.sqrt
Contingent claims	Random variable	np.arange, np.maximum, plt.plot
Replication, arbitrage	Linear equations, matrix form	ndarray(2d), np.linalg.solve, np.dot
Completeness, Arrow-Debreu securities	Linear independence, span	np.linalg.solve
Martingale pricing	Martingale, martingale measure	np.dot
Mean-variance	Expectation, variance, standard deviation	np.linspace, .std(), [x for y in z]

Economy

The first element of the financial model is the idea of an *economy*. An economy is an abstract notion that subsumes other elements of the financial model, like assets (real, financial), agents (people, institutions), or money. Like in the real world, an economy cannot be seen or touched. Nor can it be formally modeled directly—it rather simplifies communication to have such a summary term available. The single model elements together form the economy.[2]

Real Assets

Multiple *real assets* are available in the economy that can be used for different purposes. A real asset might be a chicken egg or a complex machine to produce other real assets. At this point, it is not relevant who, for example, produces the real assets or who owns them.

Agents

Agents can be thought of as individual human beings being active in the economy. They might be involved in producing real assets or consuming them or trading them. They accept money during transactions and spend it during others. An agent might

---

2 A more formal treatment of the concept of an *economy* is found in Chapter 5.

also be an institution like a bank that allows other agents to deposit money on which it then pays interest.

Time

Economic activity, like trading real assets, takes place at discrete points in time only. Formally, it holds for a point in time $t \in 0, 1, 2, 3, \ldots$ or $t \in \mathbb{N}_0$. In the following, only the two points in time $t = 0$ and $t = 1$ are relevant. They should be best interpreted as *today* and *one year from today*, although it is not necessarily the only interpretation of the relevant time interval. In many contexts, one can also think of *today* and *tomorrow*. In any case, financial theory speaks of a *static economy* if only two points in time are relevant.

The Python data type to model the natural numbers $\mathbb{N}$ is int, which stands for *integers*.[3] Typical arithmetic operations are possible on integers like addition, subtraction, multiplication, and more:

```
In [1]: 1 + 3   ❶
Out[1]: 4

In [2]: 3 * 4   ❷
Out[2]: 12

In [3]: t = 0   ❸

In [4]: t       ❹
Out[4]: 0

In [5]: t = 1   ❺

In [6]: type(t)   ❻
Out[6]: int
```

❶ Adds up two integer values.

❷ Multiplies two integer values.

❸ Assigns a value of 0 to the variable name t.

❹ Prints out the value of variable t.

---

3 For details on the standard data types in Python, refer to the Built-in Types (*https://oreil.ly/YTWep*) documentation.

❺ Assigns a new value of 1 to t.

❻ Looks up and prints the Python type of t.

Money

In the economy, *money* (or *currency*), is available in unlimited supply. Money is also infinitely divisible. Money and currency should be thought of in abstract terms only and not in terms of cash (physical coins or bills).

Money in general serves as the *numeraire* in the economy in that the value of one unit of money (think USD, EUR, GBP, etc.) is normalized to exactly 1. The prices for all other goods are then expressed in such units and are fractions or multiples of such units. Formally, units of the currency are represented as (non-negative) real numbers $c \in \mathbb{R}_{\geq 0}$.

In Python, float is the standard data type used to represent real numbers $\mathbb{R}$. It stands for *floating point numbers*. Like the int type, it allows, among others, for typical arithmetic operations, like addition and subtraction:

```
In [7]: 1 + 0.5    ❶
Out[7]: 1.5

In [8]: 10.5 - 2   ❷
Out[8]: 8.5

In [9]: c = 2 + 0.75    ❸

In [10]: c    ❹
Out[10]: 2.75

In [11]: type(c)    ❺
Out[11]: float
```

❶ Adding two numbers.

❷ Subtracting two numbers.

❸ Assigning the result of the addition to the variable c.

❹ Printing the value of the variable c.

❺ Looking up and printing out the Python type of the variable c.

Beyond serving as a numeraire, money also allows agents to buy and sell real assets or to store value over time. These two functions rest on the trust that money indeed has intrinsic value today and also in one year. In general, this translates into trust in people and institutions being willing to accept money both today and later for any kind of transaction. The numeraire function is independent of this trust since it is a numerical operation only.

Cash Flow

Combining time with currency leads to the notion of *cash flow*. Consider an investment project that requires an investment of, say, 9.5 currency units today and pays back 11.75 currency units after one year. An investment is generally considered to be a cash *outflow*, and one often represents this as a negative real number, $c \in \mathbb{R}_{<0}$, or, more specifically, $c = -9.5$. The payback is a cash *inflow* and therewith a positive real number, $c \in \mathbb{R}_{\geq 0}$, or $c = +11.75$ in the example.

To indicate the points in time when cash flows happen, a time index is used: in the example, $c_{t=0} = -9.5$ and $c_{t=1} = 11.75$, or for short, $c_0 = -9.5$ and $c_1 = 11.75$.

A pair of cash flows now and one year from now is modeled mathematically as an *ordered pair* or *two-tuple*, which combines the two relevant cash flows into one object: $c \in \mathbb{R}^2$ with $c = (c_0, c_1)$ and $c_0, c_1 \in \mathbb{R}$.

In Python, there are multiple data structures available to model such a mathematical object. The two most basic ones are tuple and list. Objects of type tuple are immutable, that is, they cannot be changed after instantiation, while those of type list are mutable and can be changed after instantiation. First, an illustration of tuple objects (characterized by parentheses):

```
In [12]: c0 = -9.5      ❶

In [13]: c1 = 11.75     ❷

In [14]: c = (c0, c1)   ❸

In [15]: c              ❹
Out[15]: (-9.5, 11.75)

In [16]: type(c)        ❺
Out[16]: tuple

In [17]: c[0]           ❻
Out[17]: -9.5

In [18]: c[1]           ❼
Out[18]: 11.75
```

❶ Defines the cash outflow today.

❷ Defines the cash inflow one year later.

❸ Defines the `tuple` object c (note the use of parentheses).

❹ Prints out the cash flow pair (note the parentheses).

❺ Looks up and shows the type of object c.

❻ Accesses the first element of object c.

❼ Accesses the second element of object c.

Second, an illustration of the `list` object (characterized by square brackets):

```
In [19]: c = [c0, c1]  ❶

In [20]: c  ❷
Out[20]: [-9.5, 11.75]

In [21]: type(c)  ❸
Out[21]: list

In [22]: c[0]  ❹
Out[22]: -9.5

In [23]: c[1]  ❺
Out[23]: 11.75

In [24]: c[0] = 10  ❻

In [25]: c  ❼
Out[25]: [10, 11.75]
```

❶ Defines the `list` object c (note the use of square brackets).

❷ Prints out the cash flow pair (note the square brackets).

❸ Looks up and shows the type of object c.

❹ Accesses the first element of object c.

❺ Accesses the second element of object c.

❻ Overwrites the value at the first index position in the object c.

❼ Shows the resulting changes.

Return

Consider an investment project with cash flows $c = (c_0, c_1) = (-10, 12)$. The *return* $R \in \mathbb{R}$ of the project is the sum of the cash flows $R = c_0 + c_1 = -10 + 12 = 2$. The *rate of return*, $r \in \mathbb{R}$, is the return, R, divided by $|c_0|$, that is by the absolute value of the investment outlay today:

$$r = \frac{R}{|c_0|} = \frac{-10 + 12}{10} = \frac{2}{10} = 0.2$$

In Python, this boils down to simple arithmetic operations:

```
In [26]: c = (-10, 12)    ❶

In [27]: R = sum(c)    ❷

In [28]: R    ❸
Out[28]: 2

In [29]: r = R / abs(c[0])    ❹

In [30]: r    ❺
Out[30]: 0.2
```

❶ Defines the cash flow pair as `tuple` object.

❷ Calculates the return R by taking the sum of all elements of c and…

❸ …prints out the result.

❹ Calculates the rate of return r with `abs(x)`, giving the absolute value of x and…

❺ …prints out the result.

Interest

There is a difference between a cash flow today and a cash flow in one year. The difference results from *interest* that is being earned on currency units or that has to be paid to borrow currency units. Interest in this context is the *price* being paid for having control over money that belongs to another agent.

An agent that has currency units that they do not need today can deposit these with a bank or lend them to another agent *to earn interest*. If the agent needs more currency units than they currently have available, they can borrow them from a bank or other agents, but they will need *to pay interest*.

Suppose an agent deposits $c_0 = -10$ currency units today with a bank. According to the deposit contract, they receive $c_1 = 11$ currency units after one year from the bank. The interest, $I \in \mathbb{R}$, being paid on the deposit is $I = c_0 + c_1 = -10 + 11 = 1$. The *interest rate*, $i \in \mathbb{R}$, accordingly is $i = \dfrac{I}{|c_0|} = 0.1$.

In the following, it is assumed that the relevant interest rate for both lending and borrowing is the same and that it is fixed for the entire economy.

Present Value

Having lending or depositing options available leads to *opportunity costs* for deploying money in an investment project. A cash flow of, say, $c_1 = 12.1$ in one year cannot be compared directly in terms of value with a cash flow of $c_0 = 12.1$ today since interest can be earned on currency units not deployed in a project.

To appropriately compare cash flows in one year with those of today, the *present value* needs to be calculated. This is accomplished by *discounting* using the fixed interest rate in the economy. Discounting can be modeled as a function $D:$ $\mathbb{R} \to \mathbb{R}, c_1 \mapsto D(c_1)$, which maps a real number (cash flow in one year) to another real number (cash flow today). It holds

$$
\begin{aligned}
c_0 &= D(c_1) \\
&= \frac{c_1}{1+i} \\
&= \frac{12.1}{1+0.1} \\
&= 11
\end{aligned}
$$

for an interest rate of $i = 0.1$. This relationship results from the alternative "investment" in deposits with a bank:

$$
c_1 = (1+i) \cdot c_0 \Longleftrightarrow c_0 = \frac{c_1}{1+i}
$$

Python functions are well suited to represent mathematical functions like the one for discounting:

```
In [31]: i = 0.1   ❶

In [32]: def D(c1):   ❷
             return c1 / (1 + i)   ❸
```

```
In [33]: D(12.1)  ❹
Out[33]: 10.999999999999998

In [34]: D(11)  ❺
Out[34]: 10.0
```

❶ Fixes the interest rate i.

❷ Function definition with def statement; D is the function name; c1 is the parameter name.

❸ Returns the present value with the return statement.

❹ Calculates the present value of 12.1; note the rounding error due to internal floating point number representation issues.

❺ Calculates the present value of 11 ("exactly" in this case).

Net Present Value

How shall an agent decide whether to conduct an investment project or not? One criterion is the *net present value*. The net present value, $NPV \in \mathbb{R}$, is the sum of the cash outflow today and the present value of the cash inflow in one year:

$$NPV(c) = c_0 + D(c_1)$$

Here, the net present value calculation is a function $NPV : \mathbb{R}^2 \to \mathbb{R}$ mapping a cash flow tuple to a real number. If the net present value is positive, the project should be conducted; if it is negative, then not—since the alternative of just depositing the money with a bank is more attractive.

Consider an investment project with cash flows $c^A = (-10.5, 12.1)$. The net present value is $NPV(c^A) = -10.5 + D(12.1) = -10.5 + 11 = 0.5$. The project should be conducted. Consider an alternative investment project with $c^B = (-10.5, 11)$. This one has a negative net present value and should not be conducted: $NPV(c^B) = -10.5 + D(11) = -10.5 + 10 = -0.5$.

Building on previous definitions, a respective Python function is easily defined:

```
In [35]: def NPV(c):
             return c[0] + D(c[1])

In [36]: cA = (-10.5, 12.1)  ❶

In [37]: cB = (-10.5, 11)  ❷
```

```
In [38]: NPV(cA)   ❶
Out[38]: 0.4999999999999982

In [39]: NPV(cB)   ❷
Out[39]: -0.5
```

❶ Positive net present value project.

❷ Negative net present value project.

Uncertainty

Cash inflows from an investment project one year from now are in general *uncertain*. They might be influenced by a number of factors in reality (competitive forces, new technologies, growth of the economy, weather, problems during project implementation, etc.). In the model economy, the concept of *states* of the economy in one year subsumes the influence of all relevant factors.

Assume that in one year the economy might be in one of two different states u and d, which might be interpreted as *up* ("good") and *down* ("bad"). The cash flow of a project in one year c_1 then becomes a *vector*

$$c_1 \in \mathbb{R}^2$$

with two different values

$$c_1^u, c_1^d \in \mathbb{R}$$

representing the relevant cash flows per state of the economy. Formally, this is represented as a so-called *column vector*:

$$c_1 = \begin{pmatrix} c_1^u \\ c_1^d \end{pmatrix}$$

Mathematically, there are certain operations defined on such vectors, like *scalar multiplication* and *addition*, for instance:

$$\alpha \cdot c_1 + \beta = \alpha \cdot \begin{pmatrix} c_1^u \\ c_1^d \end{pmatrix} + \beta = \begin{pmatrix} \alpha \cdot c_1^u + \beta \\ \alpha \cdot c_1^d + \beta \end{pmatrix}$$

Another important operation on vectors is the creation of *linear combinations* of vectors. Consider two different vectors: $c_1, d_1 \in \mathbb{R}^2$. A linear combination is then given by:

$$\alpha \cdot c_1 + \beta \cdot d_1 = \begin{pmatrix} \alpha \cdot c_1^u + \beta \cdot d_1^u \\ \alpha \cdot c_1^d + \beta \cdot d_1^d \end{pmatrix}$$

Here and before, it is assumed that $\alpha, \beta \in \mathbb{R}$.

The most common way of modeling vectors (and matrices) in Python is via the NumPy (*http://numpy.org*) package, which is an external package and needs to be installed separately. For the following code, consider an investment project with $c_0 = -10$ and $c_1 = (20, 5)^T$, where the superscript T stands for the transpose of the vector (transforming a *row or horizontal vector* into a *column or vertical vector*). The major class used to model vectors is the ndarray class, which stands for *n-dimensional array*:

```
In [40]: import numpy as np        ❶

In [41]: c0 = -10       ❷

In [42]: c1 = np.array((20, 5))        ❸

In [43]: type(c1)        ❹
Out[43]: numpy.ndarray

In [44]: c1        ❺
Out[44]: array([20,  5])

In [45]: c = (c0, c1)        ❻

In [46]: c        ❼
Out[46]: (-10, array([20,  5]))

In [47]: 1.5 * c1 + 2        ❽
Out[47]: array([32. ,  9.5])

In [48]: c1 + 1.5 * np.array((10, 4))        ❾
Out[48]: array([35., 11.])
```

❶ Imports the numpy package as np.

❷ The cash outflow today.

❸ The uncertain cash inflow in one year; one-dimensional ndarray objects do not distinguish between row (horizontal) and column (vertical).

❹ Looks up and prints the type of c1.

❺ Prints the cash flow vector.

❻ Combines the cash flows to a `tuple` object.

❼ A `tuple`, like a `list` object, can contain other complex data structures.

❽ A linear transformation of the vector by scalar multiplication and addition; technically one also speaks of a vectorized numerical operation and of broadcasting.

❾ A linear combination of two `ndarray` objects (vectors).

Financial Assets

Financial assets are financial instruments ("contracts") that have a fixed price today and an uncertain price in one year. Think of a share in the equity of a firm that conducts an investment project. Such a share might be available at a price today of $S_0 \in \mathbb{R}_{>0}$. The price of the share in one year depends on the success of the investment project, i.e., whether a high cash inflow is observed in the u state or a low one in the d state. Formally, $S_1^u, S_1^d \in \mathbb{R}_{\geq 0}$ with $S_1^u > S_1^d$.

One speaks also of the *price process* of the financial asset $S: \mathbb{N}_0 \times \{u, d\} \to \mathbb{R}_{\geq 0}$ mapping time and state of the economy to the price of the financial asset. Note that the price today is independent of the state $S_0^u = S_0^d \equiv S_0$, while the price after one year is not in general. One also writes $(S_t)_{t \in \{0, 1\}} = (S_0, S_1)$, or for short, $S = (S_0, S_1)$. The NumPy package is again the tool of choice for the modeling:

```
In [49]: S0 = 10    ❶

In [50]: S1 = np.array((12.5, 7.5))    ❷

In [51]: S = (S0, S1)    ❸

In [52]: S    ❹
Out[52]: (10, array([12.5,  7.5]))

In [53]: S[0]    ❺
Out[53]: 10

In [54]: S[1][0]    ❻
Out[54]: 12.5

In [55]: S[1][1]    ❼
Out[55]: 7.5
```

❶ The price of the financial asset today.

❷ The uncertain price in one year as a vector (`ndarray` object).

❸ The price process as a `tuple` object.

❹ Prints the price process information.

❺ Accesses the price today.

❻ Accesses the price in one year in the u (first) state.

❼ Accesses the price in one year in the d (second) state.

Risk

Often it is implicitly assumed that the two states of the economy are *equally likely*. What this means in general is that when an experiment in the economy is repeated (infinitely) many times, it is observed that half of the time the u state materializes and that in the other half the d state materializes.

This is a frequentist point of view, according to which probabilities for a state to materialize are calculated based on the frequency the state is observed divided by the total number of experiments leading to observations. If state u is observed 30 times out of 50 experiments, the probability $p \in \mathbb{R}_{\geq 0}$ with $0 \leq p \leq 1$ is accordingly $p = \frac{30}{50} = 0.6$, or 60%.

In a modeling context, the probabilities for all possible states to occur are assumed to be given *a priori*. One speaks sometimes of *objective* or *physical* probabilities.

Probability Measure

The probabilities for events that are physically possible together form a *probability measure*. Such a probability measure is a function $P: \wp(\{u, d\}) \to \mathbb{R}_{\geq 0}$ mapping all elements of the *power set* of $\{u, d\}$—with $\wp(\{u, d\}) = \{\emptyset, \{u\}, \{d\}, \{u, d\}\}$—to the unit interval. The power set in this case embodies all events that are physically possible.

In this context, the set $\{u, d\}$ is also called the *state space* and is symbolized by Ω. The triple $(\Omega, \wp(\Omega), P)$ together is called a *probability space*.

A function P representing a probability measure needs to satisfy three conditions:

1. $P(\varnothing) = 0$
2. $0 \leq P(\omega), \omega \in \Omega \leq 1$
3. $P(\Omega) = P(u) + P(d) = 1$

The first condition implies that at least one of the states must materialize. The second implies that the probability for a state to materialize is between 0 and 1. The third one says that all the probabilities add up to 1.

In the simple model economy with two states only, it is convenient to define $p \equiv P(u)$ and to accordingly have $P(d) = 1 - p$, given the preceding third condition. Fixing p then defines the probability measure P.

Having a fully specified probability measure available, the model economy is typically called an *economy under risk*. A model economy without a fully specified probability measure is often called an *economy under ambiguity*.

In applications, a probability measure is usually modeled also as a vector and `ndarray` object, respectively. This is at least possible for a discrete state space with a finite number of elements:

```
In [56]: p = 0.4
```

```
In [57]: 1 - p
Out[57]: 0.6
```

```
In [58]: P = np.array((p, 1-p))
```

```
In [59]: P
Out[59]: array([0.4, 0.6])
```

Notions of Uncertainty

Uncertainty in a financial context can take on different forms. *Risk* in general refers to a situation in which a full probability distribution over future states of the economy is (assumed to be) known. *Ambiguity* refers to situations in which such a distribution is not known. Traditionally, finance has relied almost exclusively on model economies under risk, although there is a stream of research that deals with finance problems under ambiguity (see Guidolin and Rinaldi (2012) for a survey of the research literature).

Expectation

Based on the probability measure, the *expectation* of an uncertain quantity, like the price in one year of a financial asset, can be calculated. The expectation can be interpreted as the *weighted average*, where the weights are given by the probabilities. It is an average since the probabilities add up to one.

Consider the financial asset with price process $S = (S_0, S_1)$. The expectation of the uncertain price S_1 in one year under the probability measure P is

$$\mathbf{E}^P(S_1) \equiv \sum_{\omega \in \Omega} P(\omega) \cdot S_1^\omega = p \cdot S_1^u + (1 - p) \cdot S_1^d$$

with $p \equiv P(u)$. If $S_1 = (20, 5)^T$ and $p = 0.4$ hold, the expectation value is:

$$\mathbf{E}^P(S_1) = 0.4 \cdot 20 + (1 - 0.4) \cdot 5 = 11$$

Mathematically, the expectation can be expressed as the *dot product* (or *inner product*) of two vectors. If $x, y \in \mathbb{R}^2$, the dot product is defined as

$$(x, y) = \sum_{i=1}^{2} x_i \cdot y_i = x_1 \cdot y_1 + x_2 \cdot y_2$$

Therefore, with $P = (p, 1 - p)^T$ and $S_1 = \left(S_1^u, S_1^d\right)^T$, the expectation is

$$\mathbf{E}^P(S_1) = (P, S_1) = \left(\begin{pmatrix} p \\ 1 - p \end{pmatrix}, \begin{pmatrix} S_1^u \\ S_1^d \end{pmatrix} \right) = p \cdot S_1^u + (1 - p) \cdot S_1^d$$

Working with `ndarray` objects in Python, the dot product is defined as a function provided by the NumPy package:

```
In [60]: P  ❶
Out[60]: array([0.4, 0.6])

In [61]: S0 = 10  ❷

In [62]: S1 = np.array((20, 5))  ❸

In [63]: np.dot(P, S1)  ❹
Out[63]: 11.0
```

❶ The previously defined probability measure.

❷ The price of the financial asset today.

❸ The vector of the uncertain price in one year.

❹ The dot product of the two vectors calculating the expectation value.

Expected Return

Under uncertainty, the notions of return and rate of return need to be adjusted. In such a case, the *expected return* of a financial asset is given as the expectation of the price in one year minus the price today. This can be seen by taking the expectation of the uncertain return $R = \left(R^u, R^d\right)^T$ and rearranging as follows:

$$
\begin{aligned}
\mathbf{E}^P(R) &= \left(\begin{pmatrix} p \\ 1-p \end{pmatrix}, \begin{pmatrix} R^u \\ R^d \end{pmatrix}\right) \\
&= \left(\begin{pmatrix} p \\ 1-p \end{pmatrix}, \begin{pmatrix} S_1^u - S_0 \\ S_1^d - S_0 \end{pmatrix}\right) \\
&= p \cdot \left(S_1^u - S_0\right) + (1-p) \cdot \left(S_1^d - S_0\right) \\
&= p \cdot S_1^u + (1-p) \cdot S_1^d - S_0 \\
&= \mathbf{E}^P(S_1) - S_0
\end{aligned}
$$

With the assumptions from before, one gets:

$$
\mathbf{E}^P(R) = 0.4 \cdot (20 - 10) + (1 - 0.4) \cdot (5 - 10) = 11 - 10 = 1
$$

The *expected rate of return* then simply is the expected return divided by the price today

$$
\mathbf{E}^P(r) = \frac{\mathbf{E}^P(R)}{S_0}
$$

which can also be derived step by step with similar transformations as for the expected return. In what follows, the expected rate of return is symbolized by $\mu \equiv \mathbf{E}^P(r)$ for brevity.

The calculation of expected return and rate of return can be modeled in Python by two simple functions:

```
In [64]: def ER(x0, x1):
            return np.dot(P, x1) - x0   ❶

In [65]: ER(S0, S1)   ❷
Out[65]: 1.0

In [66]: def mu(x0, x1):
            return (np.dot(P, x1) - x0) / x0   ❸

In [67]: mu(S0, S1)   ❹
Out[67]: 0.1
```

❶ Definition of expected return.

❷ The expected return for the previously defined financial asset.

❸ Definition of the expected rate of return.

❹ The expected rate of return calculated for that asset.

Volatility

In finance, *risk and expected return* is the dominating pair of concepts. Risk can be measured in many ways, while the *volatility* as measured by the standard deviation of the rates of return is probably the most common measure. In the present context, the *variance* of the return rates of a financial asset is defined by

$$
\begin{aligned}
\sigma^2(r) &= \quad \mathbf{E}^P\!\left((r - \mu)^2\right) \\
&= \left(\begin{pmatrix} p \\ 1 - p \end{pmatrix}, \begin{pmatrix} \left(r^u - \mu\right)^2 \\ \left(r^d - \mu\right)^2 \end{pmatrix}\right)
\end{aligned}
$$

with $r^\omega \equiv \left(S_1^\omega - S_0\right)/S_0, \omega \in \Omega$. The *volatility* is defined as the standard deviation of the return rates, which is the square root of the variance

$$
\sigma(r) = \sqrt{\sigma^2(r)}
$$

Python functions modeling these two risk measures are given in the following, as is a helper function to calculate the return rates vector:

```
In [68]: def r(x0, x1):
             return (x1 - x0) / x0    ❶

In [69]: r(S0, S1)    ❷
Out[69]: array([ 1. , -0.5])

In [70]: mu = np.dot(P, r(S0, S1))    ❸

In [71]: mu    ❹
Out[71]: 0.10000000000000003

In [72]: def sigma2(P, r, mu):
             return np.dot(P, (r - mu) ** 2)    ❺

In [73]: sigma2(P, r(S0, S1), mu)    ❻
Out[73]: 0.54

In [74]: def sigma(P, r, mu):
             return np.sqrt(np.dot(P, (r - mu) ** 2))    ❼

In [75]: sigma(P, r(S0, S1), mu)    ❽
Out[75]: 0.7348469228349535
```

❶ Vectorized calculation of the rates of return vector.

❷ Applies the function to the financial asset from before.

❸ The expected rate of return via the dot product…

❹ …printed out.

❺ The definition of the variance of the rates of return.

❻ The function applied to the rates of return vector.

❼ The definition of the volatility.

❽ And applied to the rates of return vector.

Vectors, Matrices, and NumPy

Finance as an applied mathematical discipline relies heavily on linear algebra and probability theory. In the discrete model economy, both mathematical disciplines can be efficiently handled in Python by using the NumPy package with its powerful ndarray object. This is not only true from a modeling point of view but also from handling, calculation, optimization, visualization, and other points of view. Basically all examples in this book will support these claims.

Contingent Claims

Suppose now that a *contingent claim* is traded in the economy. This is a financial asset —formalized by some contract—that offers a state-contingent payoff one year from now. Such a contingent claim can have an arbitrary state-contingent payoff or one that is derived from the payoff of other financial assets. In the latter case, one generally speaks of *derivative assets* or *derivative instruments*. Formally, a contingent claim is a function $C_1 : \Omega \to \mathbb{R}_{\geq 0}, \omega \mapsto C_1(\omega)$ mapping events to (non-negative) real numbers.

Assume that two financial assets are traded in the economy: a risk-less bond with price process $B = (B_0, B_1)$ and a risky stock with price process

$$S = \left(S_0, \left(S_1^u, S_1^d \right)^T \right)$$

A *call option* on the stock has a payoff in one year of $C_1(S_1(\omega)) = \max (S_1(\omega) - K, 0)$ and $\omega \in \Omega$. $K \in \mathbb{R}_{\geq 0}$ is called the *strike price* of the option.

In probability theory, a contingent claim is usually called a *random variable* whose defining characteristic is that it maps elements of the state space to real numbers— potentially via other random variables, as is the case for derivative assets. In that sense, the price of the stock in one year $S_1 : \Omega \to \mathbb{R}_{\geq 0}, \omega \mapsto S_1(\omega)$ is also a random variable.[4]

For the sake of illustration, the following Python code visualizes the payoff of a call option on a segment of the real line. In the economy, there are, of course, only two states—and therewith two values—of relevance. Figure 2-1 shows the payoff function graphically:

```
In [76]: S1 = np.arange(20)      ❶

In [77]: S1[:7]      ❷
Out[77]: array([0, 1, 2, 3, 4, 5, 6])

In [78]: K = 10      ❸

In [79]: C1 = np.maximum(S1 - K, 0)      ❹

In [80]: C1      ❺
Out[80]: array([0, 0, 0, 0, 0, 0, 0, 0, 0, 0, 0, 1, 2, 3, 4, 5, 6, 7, 8, 9])

In [81]: from pylab import mpl, plt      ❻
```

---

4 For a formal definition of a random variable, see Chapter 5.

```
# plotting configuration
plt.style.use('seaborn')
mpl.rcParams['savefig.dpi'] = 300
mpl.rcParams['font.family'] = 'serif'

In [82]: plt.figure(figsize=(10, 6))
         plt.plot(S1, C1, lw = 3.0, label='$C_1 = \max(S_1 - K, 0)$')  ❼
         plt.legend(loc=0)  ❽
         plt.xlabel('$S_1$')  ❾
         plt.ylabel('$C_1$');  ❿
```

❶   Generates an ndarray object with numbers from 0 to 19.

❷   Shows the first few numbers.

❸   Fixes the strike price for the call option.

❹   Calculates in vectorized fashion the call option payoff values.

❺   Shows these values—many values are 0.

❻   Imports the main plotting subpackage from matplotlib (*http://matplotlib.org*).

❼   Plots the call option payoff against the stock values, sets the line width to 3 pixels, and defines a label as a string object with Latex code.

❽   Puts the legend in the optimal location (least overlap with plot elements).

❾   Places a label on the x axis…

❿   …and on the y axis.

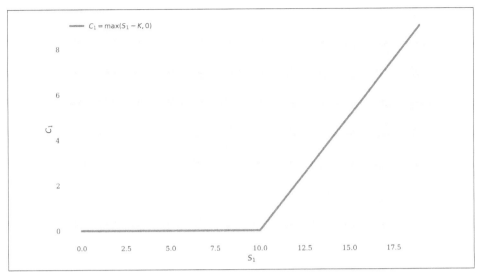

Figure 2-1. Payoff of the call option

Replication

When introducing a contingent claim into the economy, an important question that arises is whether the payoff of the contingent claim is redundant or not. Mathematically, one speaks of the payoff vector of the contingent claim being *linearly dependent* or *linearly independent*.

The payoff of the call option is said to be linearly dependent—or redundant—when a solution to the following problem exists

$$b \cdot \begin{pmatrix} B_1 \\ B_1 \end{pmatrix} + s \cdot \begin{pmatrix} S_1^u \\ S_1^d \end{pmatrix} = \begin{pmatrix} C_1^u \\ C_1^d \end{pmatrix}$$

with $b, s \in \mathbb{R}$.

This problem can be represented as a *system of linear equations*:

$$\begin{cases} b \cdot B_1 + s \cdot S_1^u = C_1^u \\ b \cdot B_1 + s \cdot S_1^d = C_1^d \end{cases}$$

With $S_1^u \neq S_1^d$, solutions are given by

$$s^\star = \frac{C_1^u - C_1^d}{S_1^u - S_1^d}$$

and

$$b^\star = \frac{1}{B_1} \frac{C_1^d \cdot S_1^u - C_1^u \cdot S_1^d}{S_1^u - S_1^d}$$

Assume as before that two financial assets are traded, a risk-less bond $B = (10, 11)$ and a risky stock $S = \left(10, (20, 5)^T\right)$. Assume further $K = 15$ such that $C_1 = (5, 0)^T$. The optimal numerical solutions are then

$$s^\star = \frac{5 - 0}{20 - 5} = \frac{1}{3}$$

and

$$b^\star = \frac{1}{11} \cdot \frac{0 \cdot 20 - 5 \cdot 5}{20 - 5} = -\frac{5}{33}$$

In words, buying one-third of the stock and selling $\frac{5}{33}$ of the bond short perfectly replicates the payoff of the call option. Therefore, the payoff of the call option is linearly dependent given the payoff vectors of the bond and the stock.

Technically, *short selling* implies borrowing the respective number of units of the financial asset today from another agent and immediately selling the units in the market. In one year, the borrowing agent buys the exact number of units of the financial asset back in the market at the then-current price and transfers them back to the other agent.

The analysis here assumes that all financial assets—like money—are infinitely divisible, which might not be the case in practice. It also assumes that short selling of all traded financial assets is possible, which might not be too unrealistic given market practice.

As a preparation for the implementation in Python, consider yet another way of formulating the replication problem. To this end, the mathematical concept of a *matrix* is needed. While a vector is a one-dimensional object, a matrix is a two-dimensional object. For the purposes of this section, consider a square matrix $\mathcal{M}$ with four elements—implying $\mathcal{M} \in \mathbb{R}^{2 \times 2}$—with

$$\mathcal{M} = \begin{pmatrix} B_1 & S_1^u \\ B_1 & S_1^d \end{pmatrix}$$

The future payoff vectors of the bond and the stock represent the values in the first and second column of the matrix, respectively. The first row contains the payoff of both financial assets in the state u, while the second row contains the payoffs from the d state. With these conventions, the replication problem can be represented in *matrix form* as

$$\mathcal{M} \cdot \phi = C_1$$

where $\phi \in \mathbb{R}^2$ is the vector containing the bond and stock portfolio positions for replication $\phi \equiv (b, s)^T$. ϕ is usually simply called a *portfolio* or *trading strategy*. Therefore:

$$\begin{pmatrix} B_1 & S_1^u \\ B_1 & S_1^d \end{pmatrix} \cdot \begin{pmatrix} b \\ s \end{pmatrix} = \begin{pmatrix} C_1^u \\ C_1^d \end{pmatrix}$$

In this context, *matrix multiplication* is defined by

$$\begin{pmatrix} B_1 & S_1^u \\ B_1 & S_1^d \end{pmatrix} \cdot \begin{pmatrix} b \\ s \end{pmatrix} \equiv \begin{pmatrix} B_1 \cdot b + S_1^u \cdot s \\ B_1 \cdot b + S_1^d \cdot s \end{pmatrix}$$

which shows the equivalence between this way of representing the replication problem and the one from before.

The ndarray class allows for a modeling of matrices in Python. The NumPy package provides in the subpackage np.linalg a wealth of functions for linear algebra operations, among which there is also a function to solve systems of linear equations in matrix form—exactly what is needed here:

```
In [83]: B = (10, np.array((11, 11)))   ❶

In [84]: S = (10, np.array((20, 5)))    ❷

In [85]: M = np.array((B[1], S[1])).T   ❸

In [86]: M                              ❹
Out[86]: array([[11, 20],
                [11,  5]])

In [87]: K = 15                         ❺
```

```
In [88]: C1 = np.maximum(S[1] - K, 0)  ❻
```

```
In [89]: C1  ❼
Out[89]: array([5, 0])
```

```
In [90]: phi = np.linalg.solve(M, C1)  ❽
```

```
In [91]: phi  ❽
Out[91]: array([-0.15151515,  0.33333333])
```

❶ Defines the price process for the risk-less bond.

❷ Defines the price process for the risky stock.

❸ Defines a matrix—i.e., a two-dimensional ndarray object—with the future payoff vectors.

❹ Shows the matrix with the numerical values.

❺ Fixes the strike price for the call option and…

❻ …calculates the values for the payoff vector in one year.

❼ Shows the numerical values of the payoff vector.

❽ Solves the replication problem in matrix form to obtain the optimal portfolio positions.

Arbitrage Pricing

How much does it cost to replicate the payoff of the call option? Once the portfolio to accomplish the replication is derived, this question is easy to answer. Define the value of the replication portfolio today by $V_0(\phi)$. It is given by the dot product

$$V_0(\phi) \equiv \left(\binom{b}{s}, \binom{B_0}{S_0} \right) = b \cdot B_0 + s \cdot S_0$$

or in numbers

$$V_0(\phi) = b \cdot B_0 + s \cdot S_0 = \frac{10}{3} - \frac{50}{33} = 1.818181$$

The uncertain value of the replication portfolio in one year $V_1(\phi)$ can be represented via matrix multiplication as

$$V_1(\phi) = \begin{pmatrix} B_1 & S_1^u \\ B_1 & S_1^d \end{pmatrix} \cdot \begin{pmatrix} b \\ s \end{pmatrix} = \begin{pmatrix} 5 \\ 0 \end{pmatrix}$$

Together, one has the *value process* of the portfolio as $V(\phi) = (V_0(\phi), V_1(\phi))$, or $V = (V_0, V_1)$ for short, if there is no ambiguity regarding the portfolio.

Having a portfolio available that perfectly replicates the future payoff of a contingent claim raises the next question: what if the price of the contingent claim today differs from the costs of setting up the replication portfolio? The answer is simple but serious: then there exists an *arbitrage* or *arbitrage opportunity* in the economy. An arbitrage is a trading strategy ϕ that creates a risk-less profit out of an investment of zero. Formally, ϕ is an arbitrage if

$$V_0(\phi) = 0 \text{ and } \mathbf{E}^P(V_1(\phi)) > 0$$

or

$$V_0(\phi) > 0 \text{ and } V_1(\phi) = 0$$

Suppose that the price of the call option is $C_0 = 2$, which is higher than the cost to set up the replication portfolio. A trading strategy that sells the call option in the market for 2 and buys the replication portfolio for 1.81818 yields an immediate profit of the difference. In one year, the payoff of the replication portfolio and of the call option cancel each other out

$$-\begin{pmatrix} C_1^u \\ C_1^d \end{pmatrix} + b^\star \begin{pmatrix} B_1 \\ B_1 \end{pmatrix} + s^\star \begin{pmatrix} S_1^u \\ S_1^d \end{pmatrix} = \begin{pmatrix} 0 \\ 0 \end{pmatrix}$$

by the definition of the replication portfolio. In the other case, when the price of the call option today is lower than the price of the replication portfolio, say $C_0 = 1.5$, a trading strategy buying the call option and selling the replication portfolio yields a risk-less profit amounting to the difference between the market price of the call option and the cost to set up the replication portfolio. Of course, the risk-less profits in both cases can be increased by simply multiplying the positions by a positive factor greater than one.

A model for an economy that allows for arbitrage opportunities can be considered not viable. Therefore, the only price that is consistent with the absence of arbitrage is $C_0 = 1.818181$. One calls this price the *arbitrage price* of the call option. Whenever there is a portfolio ϕ replicating the payoff of a contingent claim $V_1(\phi) = C_1$, then the arbitrage price of the contingent claim is $C_0 = V_0(\phi)$.

Formally, the arbitrage price is the dot product of the replication portfolio and the price vector of the replicating financial assets

$$C_0 \equiv V_0(\phi) = \left(\phi^*, \begin{pmatrix} B_0 \\ S_0 \end{pmatrix} \right) = b^* \cdot B_0 + s^* \cdot S_0$$

giving rise to an arbitrage-free price process for the contingent claim of $C = (C_0, C_1)$.

In Python, this is a single calculation given the previous definitions and calculations:

```
In [92]: C0 = np.dot(phi, (B[0], S[0]))
```

```
In [93]: C0
Out[93]: 1.8181818181818183
```

```
In [94]: 10/3 - 50/33
Out[94]: 1.8181818181818183
```

Market Completeness

Does arbitrage pricing work for every contingent claim? Yes, at least for those that are replicable by portfolios of financial assets that are traded in the economy. The *set of attainable contingent claims* $\mathbb{A}$ comprises all those contingent claims that are replicable by trading in the financial assets. It is given by the *span*, which is the set of all linear combinations of the future price vectors of the traded financial assets

$$\mathbb{A} = \left\{ \mathcal{M} \cdot \phi, \phi \in \mathbb{R}_{\geq 0}^2 \right\}$$

if short-selling is prohibited and

$$\mathbb{A} = \left\{ \mathcal{M} \cdot \phi, \phi \in \mathbb{R}^2 \right\}$$

if it is allowed in unlimited fashion.

Consider the risk-less bond and the risky stock from before with price processes $B = (B_0, B_1)$ and $S = \left(S_0, \left(S_1^u, S_1^d \right)^T \right)$, respectively, where $B_1, S_1 \in \mathbb{R}_{\geq 0}^2$ and $S_1^u \neq S_1^d$. It is then easy to show that the replication problem

$$\mathcal{M} \cdot \phi = C_1$$

has a unique solution for any $C_1 \in \mathbb{R}^2_{\geq 0}$. The solution is given by

$$\phi^\star = \begin{pmatrix} b^\star \\ s^\star \end{pmatrix}$$

and consequently as

$$\phi^\star = \begin{pmatrix} \dfrac{1}{B_1} \dfrac{C_1^d \cdot S_1^u - C_1^u \cdot S_1^d}{S_1^u - S_1^d} \\[3mm] \dfrac{C_1^u - C_1^d}{S_1^u - S_1^d} \end{pmatrix}$$

which was derived in the context of the replication of the special call option payoff. The solution carries over to the general case since no special assumptions have been made regarding the payoff other than $C_1 \in \mathbb{R}^2_{\geq 0}$.

Since *every* contingent claim can be replicated by a portfolio consisting of a position in the risk-less bond and the risky stock, one speaks of a *complete market model*. Therefore, every contingent claim can be priced by replication and arbitrage. Formally, the only requirement is that the price vectors of the two financial assets in one year be linearly independent. This implies that

$$\begin{pmatrix} B_1 & S_1^u \\ B_1 & S_1^d \end{pmatrix} \cdot \begin{pmatrix} b \\ s \end{pmatrix} = \begin{pmatrix} 0 \\ 0 \end{pmatrix}$$

has only the unique solution $\phi^\star = (0, 0)^T$ and no other solution. In fact, all replication problems for arbitrary contingent claims have unique solutions under market completeness. The payoff vectors of the two traded financial assets span the $\mathbb{R}^2$ since they form a *basis* of the *vector space* $\mathbb{R}^2$.

The spanning property can be visualized by the use of Python and the `matplotlib` (*https://matplotlib.org*) package. To this end, 1,000 random portfolio compositions are simulated. The first restriction is that the portfolio positions should be positive and add up to 1. Figure 2-2 shows the result:

```
In [95]: from numpy.random import default_rng
         rng = default_rng(100)  ❶

In [96]: n = 1000  ❷

In [97]: b = rng.random(n)  ❸

In [98]: b[:5]  ❸
Out[98]: array([0.83498163, 0.59655403, 0.28886324, 0.04295157, 0.9736544 ])

In [99]: s = (1 - b)  ❹

In [100]: s[:5]  ❹
Out[100]: array([0.16501837, 0.40344597, 0.71113676, 0.95704843, 0.0263456 ])

In [101]: def portfolio(b, s):
              A = [b[i] * B[1] + s[i] * S[1] for i in range(n)]  ❺
              return np.array(A)  ❻

In [102]: A = portfolio(b, s)  ❼

In [103]: A[:3]  ❼
Out[103]: array([[12.48516533, 10.00988978],
                 [14.63101376,  8.57932416],
                 [17.40023082,  6.73317945]])

In [104]: plt.figure(figsize=(10, 6))
          plt.plot(A[:, 0], A[:, 1], 'r.');  ❽
```

❶ Fixes the seed for the random number generator.

❷ Number of values to be simulated.

❸ Simulates the bond position for values between 0 and 1 by the means of a uniform distribution.

❹ Derives the stock position as the difference between 1 and the bond position.

❺ Calculates the portfolio payoff vectors for all random portfolio compositions and collects them in a list object; this Python idiom is called a list comprehension.

❻ The function returns an ndarray version of the results.

❼ The calculation is initiated.

❽ The results are plotted.

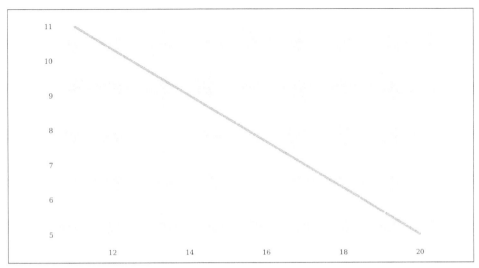

Figure 2-2. The random portfolios spanning a one-dimensional line only

Figure 2-3 shows the graphical results in the case where the portfolio positions do not need to add up to 1:

```
In [105]: s = rng.random(n)  ❶

In [106]: b[:5] + s[:5]
Out[106]: array([1.36885777, 1.5863474 , 0.71245805, 0.32077672, 1.5401562 ])

In [107]: A = portfolio(b, s)  ❷

In [108]: plt.figure(figsize=(10, 6))
          plt.plot(A[:, 0], A[:, 1], 'r.');
```

❶ The stock position is freely simulated for values between 0 and 1.

❷ The portfolio payoff vectors are calculated.

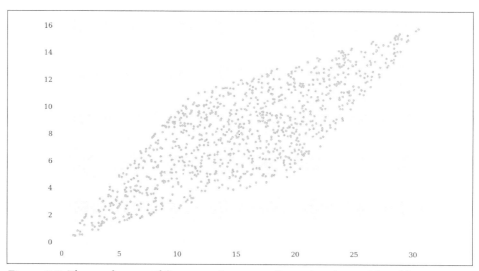

Figure 2-3. The random portfolios spanning a two-dimensional area (rhomb)

Finally, Figure 2-4 allows for positive as well as negative portfolio positions for both the bond and the stock. The resulting portfolio payoff vectors cover an (elliptic) area around the origin:

```
In [109]: b = rng.standard_normal(n)  ❶

In [110]: s = rng.standard_normal(n)  ❶

In [111]: b[:5] + s[:5]  ❶
Out[111]: array([-0.23046605, -3.45760465,  1.10260637, -2.44445777,
          1.05866637])

In [112]: A = portfolio(b, s)

In [113]: plt.figure(figsize=(10, 6))
          plt.plot(A[:, 0], A[:, 1], 'r.');
```

❶ Positive and negative portfolio positions are simulated by the means of the standard normal distribution.

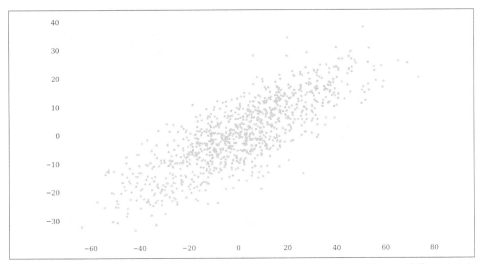

Figure 2-4. The random portfolios spanning a two-dimensional area (around the origin)

If b and s are allowed to take on arbitrary values on the real line, $b, s \in \mathbb{R}$, the resulting portfolios cover the vector space $\mathbb{R}^2$ completely. As pointed out previously, the payoff vectors of the traded financial assets span $\mathbb{R}^2$ in that case.

Arrow-Debreu Securities

An *Arrow-Debreu security* is defined by the fact that it pays exactly one unit of currency in a specified future state. In a model economy with two different future states only, there can only be two different such securities. An Arrow-Debreu security is simply a special case of a contingent claim such that the replication argument from before applies. In other words, since the market is complete, Arrow-Debreu securities can be replicated by portfolios in the bond and stock. Therefore, both replication problems have (unique) solutions, and both securities have unique arbitrage prices. The two replication problems are

$$\mathcal{M} \cdot \phi = \begin{pmatrix} 1 \\ 0 \end{pmatrix}$$

and

$$\mathcal{M} \cdot \phi = \begin{pmatrix} 0 \\ 1 \end{pmatrix}$$

Why are these securities important? Mathematically, the two payoff vectors form a *standard basis* or *natural basis* for the $\mathbb{R}^2$ vector space. This in turn implies that any vector of this space can be uniquely expressed (replicated) as a linear combination of the vectors that form the standard basis. Financially, replacing the original future price vectors of the bond and the stock with Arrow-Debreu securities as a basis for the model economy significantly simplifies the replication problem for all other contingent claims.

The process is to first derive the replication portfolios for the two Arrow-Debreu securities and the resulting arbitrage prices for both. Other contingent claims are then replicated and priced based on the standard basis and the arbitrage prices of the two securities.

Consider the two Arrow-Debreu securities with price processes $\gamma^u = \left(\gamma_0^u, (1,0)^T\right)$ and $\gamma^d = \left(\gamma_0^d, (0,1)^T\right)$ and define:

$$M^\gamma = \begin{pmatrix} 1 & 0 \\ 0 & 1 \end{pmatrix}$$

Consider a general contingent claim with future payoff vector:

$$C_1 = \begin{pmatrix} C_1^u \\ C_1^d \end{pmatrix}$$

The replication portfolio ϕ^γ for the contingent claim then is trivially given by $\phi^\gamma = \left(C_1^u, C_1^d\right)^T$ since:

$$
\begin{aligned}
V_1(\phi^\gamma) &= \mathcal{M}^\gamma \cdot \phi^\gamma \\
&= \begin{pmatrix} 1 & 0 \\ 0 & 1 \end{pmatrix} \cdot \begin{pmatrix} C_1^u \\ C_1^d \end{pmatrix} \\
&= \begin{pmatrix} C_1^u \\ C_1^d \end{pmatrix}
\end{aligned}
$$

Consequently, the arbitrage price for the contingent claim is:

$$C_0 = V_0(\phi^\gamma) = C_1^u \cdot \gamma_0^u + C_1^d \cdot \gamma_0^d$$

This illustrates how the introduction of Arrow-Debreu securities simplifies contingent claim replication and arbitrage pricing.

Martingale Pricing

A *martingale measure* $Q: \wp(\Omega) \to \mathbb{R}_{\geq 0}$ is a special kind of probability measure. It makes the discounted price process of a financial asset a *martingale*. For the stock to be a martingale under Q, the following relationship must hold:

$$S_0 = \frac{1}{1+i} \cdot \mathbf{E}^Q(S_1)$$

If $i = \frac{B_1 - B_0}{B_0}$, the relationship is trivially satisfied for the risk-less bond:

$$B_0 = \frac{1}{1+i} \cdot \mathbf{E}^Q(B_1) = \frac{1}{1+i} \cdot B_1$$

One also speaks of the fact that the price processes drift (on average) with the risk-less interest rate under the martingale measure:

$$\begin{cases} B_0 \cdot (1+i) = B_1 \\ S_0 \cdot (1+i) = \mathbf{E}^Q(S_1) \end{cases}$$

Denote $q \equiv Q(u)$. One gets

$$q \cdot S_1^u + (1-q) \cdot S_1^d = S_0 \cdot (1+i)$$

or after some simple manipulations:

$$q = \frac{S_0 \cdot (1+i) - S_1^d}{S_1^u - S_1^d}$$

Given previous assumptions, for q to define a valid probability measure, $S_1^u > S_0 \cdot (1+i) > S_1^d$ must hold. If so, one gets a new probability space $(\Omega, \wp(\Omega), Q)$, where Q replaces P.

What if these relationships for S_1 do not hold? Then a *simple arbitrage* is either to buy the risky asset in the case $S_0 \cdot (1 + i) \leq S_1^d$ or simply sell it in the other case, $S_0 \cdot (1 + i) \geq S_1^u$.

If equality holds in these relationships, one also speaks of a *weak arbitrage* since the risk-less profit can only be expected on average and not with certainty.

Assuming the numerical price processes from before, the calculation of q in Python means just an arithmetic operation on floating point numbers:

```
In [114]: i = (B[1][0] - B[0]) / B[0]

In [115]: i
Out[115]: 0.1

In [116]: q = (S[0] * (1 + i) - S[1][1]) / (S[1][0] - S[1][1])

In [117]: q
Out[117]: 0.4
```

First Fundamental Theorem of Asset Pricing

The considerations at the end of the previous section hint to a relationship between martingale measures on the one hand and arbitrage on the other. A central result in mathematical finance that relates these seemingly unrelated concepts formally is the *First Fundamental Theorem of Asset Pricing*. Pioneering work in this regard has been published by Cox and Ross (1976), Harrison and Kreps (1979), and Harrison and Pliska (1981).

First Fundamental Theorem of Asset Pricing (1FTAP)
    The following statements are equivalent:

  1. A martingale measure exists.

  2. The economy is arbitrage-free.

Given the calculations and the discussion from before, the theorem is easy to prove for the model economy with the risk-less bond and the risky stock.

First, statement 1 implies statement 2: if the martingale measure exists, the price processes do not allow for simple (weak) arbitrages. Since the two future price vectors are linearly independent, every contingent claim can be replicated by trading in the two financial assets, implying unique arbitrage prices. Therefore, no arbitrages exist.

Second, statement 2 implies statement 1: if the model economy is arbitrage-free, a martingale measure exists, as shown previously.

Pricing by Expectation

A corollary of the 1FTAP is that any attainable contingent claim $C_1 \in \mathbb{A}$ can be priced by taking the expectation under the martingale measure of its future payoff and discounting with the risk-less interest rate. The arbitrage price of the call option is known through replication. Assuming the same numerical price processes for the traded financial assets and the same numerical future payoff vector for the call option, the *martingale price* of the call option is:

$$
\begin{aligned}
C_0 &= \frac{1}{1+i} \cdot \mathbf{E}^Q(C_1) \\
&= \frac{1}{1+i} \cdot \left(q \cdot C_1^u + (1-q) \cdot C_1^d \right) \\
&= \frac{1}{1+0.1} \cdot (0.4 \cdot 5 + (1-0.4) \cdot 0) \\
&= 1.818181
\end{aligned}
$$

In other words, the discounted price process of the call option—and any other contingent claim—is a martingale under the martingale measure such that:

$$
\begin{cases}
B_0 \cdot (1+i) = B_1 \\
S_0 \cdot (1+i) = \mathbf{E}^Q(S_1) \\
C_0 \cdot (1+i) = \mathbf{E}^Q(C_1)
\end{cases}
$$

In Python, martingale pricing boils down to the evaluation of a dot product:

```
In [118]: Q = (q, 1 - q)   ❶

In [119]: np.dot(Q, C1) / (1 + i)   ❷
Out[119]: 1.8181818181818181
```

❶ Defines the martingale measure as the tuple Q.

❷ Implements the martingale pricing formula.

Second Fundamental Theorem of Asset Pricing

There is another important result, often called the *Second Fundamental Theorem of Asset Pricing*, which relates the uniqueness of the martingale measure with market completeness.

Second Fundamental Theorem of Asset Pricing (2FTAP)
  The following statements are equivalent:

1. The martingale measure is unique.

2. The market model is complete.

The result also follows for the simple model economy from previous discussions. A more detailed analysis of market completeness takes place in Chapter 3.

Mean-Variance Portfolios

A major breakthrough in finance has been the formalization and quantification of portfolio investing through the *mean-variance portfolio theory* (MVP) as pioneered by Markowitz (1952). To some extent this approach can be considered to be the beginning of quantitative finance, initiating a trend that brought more and more mathematics to the financial field.

MVP reduces a financial asset to the first and second moment of its returns, namely the *mean* as the expected rate of return and the *variance* of the rates of return or the *volatility*, defined as the standard deviation of the rates of return. Although the approach is generally called "mean-variance," it is often the combination "mean-volatility" that is used.

Consider the risk-less bond and risky stock from before with price processes $B = (B_0, B_1)$ and $S = \left(S_0, \left(S_1^u, S_1^d\right)^T\right)$ and the future price matrix $\mathcal{M}$, for which the two columns are given by the future price vectors of the two financial assets. What is the expected rate of return and the volatility of a portfolio ϕ that consists of b percent invested in the bond and s percent invested the stock? Note that now a situation is assumed for which $b + s = 1$, with $b, s \in \mathbb{R}_{\geq 0}$, holds. This can, of course, be relaxed but simplifies the exposition in this section.

The *expected portfolio payoff* is:

$$
\begin{aligned}
\mathbf{E}^P(\mathcal{M} \cdot \phi) &= \quad p \cdot \left(b \cdot B_1 + s \cdot S_1^u\right) + (1 - p) \cdot \left(b \cdot B_1 + s \cdot S_1^d\right) \\
&= p \cdot \left(b \cdot B_1\right) + (1 - p) \cdot \left(b \cdot B_1\right) + p \cdot \left(s \cdot S_1^u\right) + (1 - p)\left(s \cdot S_1^d\right) \\
&= \quad\quad\quad\quad b \cdot \mathbf{E}^P(B_1) + s \cdot \mathbf{E}^P(S_1) \\
&= \quad\quad\quad\quad b \cdot B_1 + s \cdot \mathbf{E}^P(S_1)
\end{aligned}
$$

In words, the expected portfolio payoff is simply b times the risk-less bond payoff plus s times the expected stock payoff.

Defining $\mathscr{R} \in \mathbb{R}^{2 \times 2}$ to be the *rates of return matrix* with

$$\mathscr{R} = \begin{pmatrix} i & r_1^u \\ i & r_1^d \end{pmatrix}$$

one gets for the expected portfolio rate of return

$$\begin{aligned} \mathbf{E}^P(\mathscr{R} \cdot \phi) &= b \cdot \mathbf{E}^P(i) + s \cdot \mathbf{E}^P(r_1) \\ &= b \cdot i + s \cdot \mu \end{aligned}$$

In words, the expected portfolio rate of return is b times the risk-less interest rate plus s times the expected rate of return of the stock.

The next step is to calculate the *portfolio variance*:

$$\begin{aligned} \sigma^2(\mathscr{R} \cdot \phi) &= \mathbb{E}^P\left(\left(r - \mathbf{E}^P(\mathscr{R} \cdot \phi)\right)^2\right) \\ &= \left(\begin{pmatrix} p \\ 1-p \end{pmatrix}, \begin{pmatrix} \left(b \cdot i + s \cdot r_1^u - b \cdot i - s \cdot \mu\right)^2 \\ \left(b \cdot i + s \cdot r_1^d - b \cdot i - s \cdot \mu\right)^2 \end{pmatrix}\right) \\ &= \left(\begin{pmatrix} p \\ 1-p \end{pmatrix}, \begin{pmatrix} \left(s \cdot r_1^u - s \cdot \mu\right)^2 \\ \left(s \cdot r_1^d - s \cdot \mu\right)^2 \end{pmatrix}\right) \\ &= s^2 \cdot \sigma^2(r_1) \end{aligned}$$

In words, the portfolio variance is s^2 times the stock variance, which makes intuitive sense since the bond is risk-less and should not contribute to the portfolio variance. It immediately follows the nice proportionality result for the *portfolio volatility*:

$$\begin{aligned} \sigma(\mathscr{R} \cdot \phi) &= \sqrt{\sigma^2(\mathscr{R} \cdot \phi)} \\ &= \sqrt{s^2 \cdot \sigma^2(r_1)} \\ &= s \cdot \sigma(r_1) \end{aligned}$$

The whole analysis is straightforward to implement in Python. First, some preliminaries:

```
In [120]: B = (10, np.array((11, 11)))

In [121]: S = (10, np.array((20, 5)))

In [122]: M = np.array((B[1], S[1])).T  ❶

In [123]: M  ❶
Out[123]: array([[11, 20],
                 [11,  5]])

In [124]: M0 = np.array((B[0], S[0]))  ❷

In [125]: R = M / M0 - 1  ❸

In [126]: R  ❹
Out[126]: array([[ 0.1,  1. ],
                 [ 0.1, -0.5]])

In [127]: P = np.array((0.5, 0.5))  ❺
```

❶ The matrix with the future prices of the financial assets.

❷ The vector with the prices of the financial assets today.

❸ Calculates in vectorized fashion the return matrix.

❹ Shows the results of the calculation.

❺ Defines the probability measure.

With these definitions, expected portfolio return and volatility are calculated as dot products:

```
In [128]: np.dot(P, R)  ❶
Out[128]: array([0.1 , 0.25])

In [129]: s = 0.55  ❷

In [130]: phi = (1-s, s)  ❸

In [131]: mu = np.dot(phi, np.dot(P, R))  ❹

In [132]: mu  ❺
Out[132]: 0.18250000000000005

In [133]: sigma = s * R[:, 1].std()  ❻

In [134]: sigma  ❼
Out[134]: 0.41250000000000003
```

❶ The expected returns of the bond and the stock.

❷ An example allocation for the stock in percent (decimals).

❸ The resulting portfolio with a normalized weight of 1.

❹ The expected portfolio return given the allocations.

❺ The value lies between the risk-less return and the stock return.

❻ The volatility of the portfolio; the Python code here only applies due to $p = 0.5$.

❼ Again, the value lies between the volatility of the bond ($= 0$) and the volatility of the stock ($= 0.75$).

Varying the weight of the stock in the portfolio leads to different risk-return combinations. Figure 2-5 shows the expected portfolio return and volatility for different values of s between 0 and 1. As the plot illustrates, both the expected portfolio return (from 0.1 to 0.25) and the volatility (from 0.0 to 0.75) increase linearly with increasing allocation s of the stock:

```
In [135]: values = np.linspace(0, 1, 25)   ❶

In [136]: mu = [np.dot(((1-s), s), np.dot(P, R))
                  for s in values]   ❷

In [137]: sigma = [s * R[:, 1].std() for s in values]   ❸

In [138]: plt.figure(figsize=(10, 6))
          plt.plot(values, mu, lw = 3.0, label='$\mu_p$')
          plt.plot(values, sigma, '--', lw = 3.0, label='$\sigma_p$')
          plt.legend(loc=0)
          plt.xlabel('$s$');
```

❶ Generates an ndarray object with 24 evenly spaced intervals between 0 and 1.

❷ Calculates for every element in values the expected portfolio return and stores them in a list object.

❸ Calculates for every element in values the portfolio volatility and stores them in another list object.

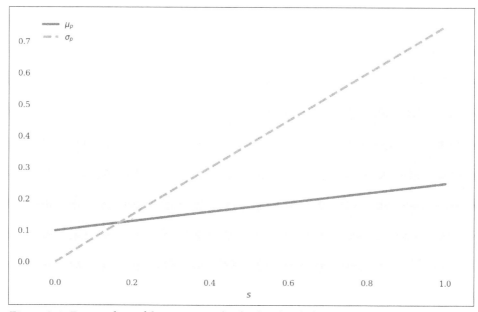

Figure 2-5. Expected portfolio return and volatility for different allocations

Note that the list comprehension `sigma = [s * R[:, 1].std() for s in values]` in the previous code is short for the following code[5]:

```
sigma = list()
for s in values:
    sigma.append(s * R[:, 1].std())
```

The typical graphic seen in the context of MVP is one that plots expected portfolio return against portfolio volatility. Figure 2-6 shows that an investor can expect a higher return the more risk (volatility) they are willing to bear. The relationship is linear in the special case of this section:

```
In [139]: plt.figure(figsize=(10, 6))
          plt.plot(sigma, mu, lw = 3.0, label='risk-return')
          plt.legend(loc=0)
          plt.xlabel('$\sigma_p$')
          plt.ylabel('$\mu_p$');
```

---

5 Refer to the Data Structures documentation (*https://oreil.ly/0dbCi*) for more on data structures and comprehension idioms in Python.

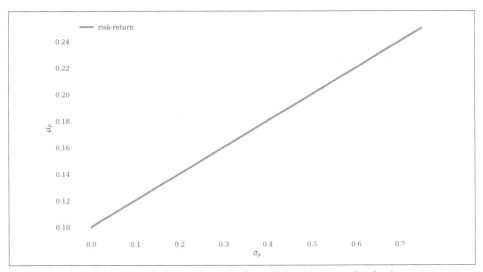

Figure 2-6. Feasible combinations of expected portfolio return and volatility

Conclusions

This chapter introduces finance, starting with the very basics and illustrating the central mathematical objects and financial notions with simple Python code examples. The beauty is that fundamental ideas of finance—like arbitrage pricing or the risk-return relationship—can be introduced and understood even in a static two-state economy. Equipped with this basic understanding and some financial and mathematical intuition, the transition to increasingly more realistic financial models is significantly simplified. The subsequent chapter, for example, adds a third future state to the state space to discuss issues arising in the context of market incompleteness.

Further Resources

Books and papers cited in this chapter:

Cox, John and Stephen Ross. 1976. "The Valuation of Options for Alternative Stochastic Processes." *Journal of Financial Economics* (3): 145–166.

Delbaen, Freddy and Walter Schachermayer. 2006. *The Mathematics of Arbitrage*. Berlin: Springer Verlag.

Guidolin, Massimo and Francesca Rinaldi. 2013. "Ambiguity in Asset Pricing and Portfolio Choice: A Review of the Literature." *Theory and Decision* (74): 183–217. *https://ssrn.com/abstract=1673494*.

Harrison, Michael and David Kreps. 1979. "Martingales and Arbitrage in Multiperiod Securities Markets." *Journal of Economic Theory* (20): 381–408.

Harrison, Michael and Stanley Pliska. 1981. "Martingales and Stochastic Integrals in the Theory of Continuous Trading." *Stochastic Processes and their Applications* (11): 215–260.

Markowitz, Harry. 1952. "Portfolio Selection." *Journal of Finance* 7 (1): 77–91.

Three-State Economy

The model is said to be *complete* if every contingent claim can be generated by some trading strategy. Otherwise, the model is said to be *incomplete*.

—Stanley Pliska (1997)

Assume that an individual views the outcome of any investment in probabilistic terms; that is, he thinks of the possible results in terms of some probability distribution. In assessing the desirability of a particular investment, however, he is willing to act on the basis of only two parameters of this distribution—its expected value and standard deviation.

—William Sharpe (1964)

The previous chapter is based on the most simple model economy, in which the notion of uncertainty in finance can be analyzed. This chapter enriches the two-state economy by just a single additional state while keeping the number of traded financial assets constant at two. In this slightly enriched *static three-state economy*, the notions of market incompleteness and indeterminacy of the martingale measure are discussed. Super-replication and approximate replication approaches are presented to cope with incompleteness and its consequences for the pricing of contingent claims. The chapter also presents the Capital Asset Pricing Model (CAPM), which builds on the mean-variance portfolio analysis and adds equilibrium arguments to derive prices for financial assets in mean-volatility space even if they are not replicable.

This chapter mainly covers the following topics from finance, mathematics, and Python programming:

Finance	Mathematics	Python
Uncertainty	Probability space	`ndarray`
Financial assets	Vectors, matrices	`ndarray`
Attainable contingent claims	Span of vectors, basis of vector space	`ndarray`
Martingale pricing, arbitrage	Sets of probability measures, expectation	`ndarray`, `np.dot`
Super-replication	Minimization, constraints	`scipy.optimize.minimize`, `dict`, `lambda`
Approximate replication	Mean squared error, OLS regression	`np.linalg.lstsq`
Capital market line	Expectation, standard deviation	`NumPy`
Capital Asset Pricing Model	Correlation, covariance	`NumPy`

If not explicitly stated otherwise, the assumptions and notions of the two-state economy from the previous chapter carry over to the three-state economy discussed in this chapter.

Uncertainty

Two *points in time* are relevant, today, $t = 0$, and one year from today in the future, $t = 1$. Let the *state space* be given by $\Omega = \{u, m, d\}$. $\{u, m, d\}$ represent the three different states of the economy possible in one year. The *power set* over the state space is given as:

$$\wp(\Omega) = \{\varnothing, \{u\}, \{m\}, \{d\}, \{u, m\}, \{u, d\}, \{m, d\}, \Omega\}$$

The probability measure P is defined on the power set, and it is assumed that $P(\omega) = \frac{1}{3}, \omega \in \Omega$. The resulting *probability space* $(\Omega, \wp(\Omega), P)$ represents *uncertainty* in the model economy.

Financial Assets

There are two financial assets traded in the model economy. The first is a *risk-less bond* $B = (B_0, B_1)$ with $B_0 = 10$ and $B_1 = (11, 11, 11)^T$. The risk-less interest rate accordingly is $i = 0.1$.

The second is a *risky stock*, $S = \left(S_0, \left(S_1^u, S_1^m, S_1^d\right)^T\right)$, with $S_0 = 10$ and:

$$S_1 = \begin{pmatrix} 20 \\ 10 \\ 5 \end{pmatrix}$$

Define the market payoff matrix $\mathcal{M} \in \mathbb{R}^{3 \times 2}$ by:

$$\mathcal{M} \equiv \begin{pmatrix} B_1 & S_1^u \\ B_1 & S_1^m \\ B_1 & S_1^d \end{pmatrix} = \begin{pmatrix} 11 & 20 \\ 11 & 10 \\ 11 & 5 \end{pmatrix}$$

Attainable Contingent Claims

The *span* of the traded financial assets is also called the *set of attainable contingent claims* $\mathbb{A}$. A contingent claim $C_1 : \Omega \to \mathbb{R}_{\geq 0}$ is said to be attainable if its payoff can be expressed as a linear combination of the payoff vectors of the traded assets. In other words, there exists a portfolio ϕ such that $V_1(\phi) = \mathcal{M} \cdot \phi = C_1$. Therefore

$$\mathbb{A} = \left\{ \mathcal{M} \cdot \phi, \phi \in \mathbb{R}^2 \right\}$$

if there are no constraints on the portfolio positions, or

$$\mathbb{A} = \left\{ \mathcal{M} \cdot \phi, \phi \in \mathbb{R}_{\geq 0}^2 \right\}$$

if short selling is prohibited.

It is easy to verify that the payoff vectors of the two financial assets are linearly independent. However, there are only two such vectors and three different states. It is known by standard results from linear algebra that a basis for the vector space $\mathbb{R}^3$ needs to consist of three linearly independent vectors. In other words, not every contingent claim is replicable by a portfolio of the traded financial assets. An example is, for instance, the *first Arrow-Debreu security*. The system of linear equations for the replication is:

$$\begin{cases} b \cdot 11 + s \cdot 20 = 1 \\ b \cdot 11 + s \cdot 10 = 0 \\ b \cdot 11 + s \cdot 5 = 0 \end{cases}$$

Subtracting the second equation from the first gives $s = \frac{1}{10}$. Subtracting the third equation from the first gives $s = \frac{1}{15}$, which is obviously a contradiction to the first result. Therefore, there is no solution to this replication problem.

Using Python, the set of attainable contingent claims can be visualized in three dimensions. The approach is based on Monte Carlo simulation for the portfolio composition. For simplicity, the simulation allows only for positive portfolio positions between 0 and 1. Figure 3-1 shows the results graphically and illustrates that the two vectors can only span a two-dimensional area of the three-dimensional space. If the market would be complete, the simulated payoff vectors would populate a cube (the financial assets would span $\mathbb{R}^3$) and not only a rectangular area (span $\mathbb{R}^2$). The modeling of uncertainty is along the lines of the Python code introduced in Chapter 2 with the necessary adjustments for three possible future states of the economy:

```
In [1]: import numpy as np
        from numpy.random import default_rng
        np.set_printoptions(precision=5, suppress=True)

In [2]: rng = default_rng(100)

In [3]: B = (10, np.array((11, 11, 11)))

In [4]: S = (10, np.array((20, 10, 5)))

In [5]: n = 1000   ❶

In [6]: b = rng.random(n)   ❷

In [7]: b[:5]   ❷
Out[7]: array([0.83498, 0.59655, 0.28886, 0.04295, 0.97365])

In [8]: s = rng.random(n)   ❸

In [9]: A = [b[i] * B[1] + s[i] * S[1] for i in range(n)]   ❹

In [10]: A = np.array(A)   ❹

In [11]: A[:3]   ❹
Out[11]: array([[19.86232, 14.52356, 11.85418],
               [26.35796, 16.46003, 11.51106],
               [11.64939,  7.41344,  5.29547]])

In [12]: from pylab import mpl, plt   ❺
         plt.style.use('seaborn')
         mpl.rcParams['savefig.dpi'] = 300
         mpl.rcParams['font.family'] = 'serif'
         from mpl_toolkits.mplot3d import Axes3D   ❻

In [13]: fig = plt.figure(figsize=(10, 6))   ❼
         ax = fig.add_subplot(111, projection='3d')   ❽
         ax.scatter(A[:, 0], A[:, 1], A[:, 2], c='r', marker='.');   ❾
```

❶ Number of portfolios to be simulated.

❷ The random position in the bond with some examples—all position values are between 0 and 1.

❸ The random position in the stock.

❹ A `list` comprehension that calculates the resulting payoff vectors from the random portfolio compositions.

❺ The basic plotting subpackage of `matplotlib`.

❻ Three-dimensional plotting capabilities.

❼ An empty canvas is created.

❽ A subplot for a three-dimensional object is added.

❾ The payoff vectors are visualized as a red dot each.

Market Incompleteness

While in a complete model economy *every* contingent claim is attainable, only a *small subset* of contingent claims is generally attainable in an incomplete market. In that sense, changing from a complete to an incomplete model economy has tremendous consequences. Pricing by replication, as introduced in Chapter 2, relies on the attainability of a contingent claim. What about pricing, then, when replication fails? These and other questions in this context are answered in the remainder of the chapter.

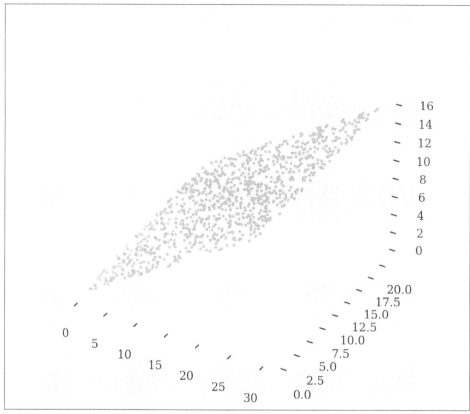

Figure 3-1. Random portfolio payoff vectors visualized in three dimensions

Martingale Pricing

The importance of martingale measures is clear from the First Fundamental Theorem of Asset Pricing (1FTAP) and the Second Fundamental Theorem of Asset Pricing (2FTAP).

Martingale Measures

Any probability measure makes the discounted bond price process a martingale. What about the stock price process? The defining equation for a martingale measure $Q: \wp(\Omega) \to \mathbb{R}_{\geq 0}$ is:

$$S_0 \cdot (1 + i) = \mathbf{E}^Q(S_1)$$

or

$$S_0 \cdot (1 + i) = q^u \cdot S_1^u + q^m \cdot S_1^m + q^d \cdot S_1^d$$

with $q^\omega \equiv Q(\omega), \omega \in \Omega$. In numbers and with $q^d = 1 - q^u - q^m$:

$$11 \quad = q^u \cdot 20 + q^m \cdot 10 + \left(1 - q^u - q^m\right) \cdot 5$$

$$\Longleftrightarrow q^m = \quad \frac{6 - 15 \cdot q^u}{5}$$

Recalling the properties of a probability measure, it must hold (binding condition)

$$6 - 15 \cdot q^u \geq 0$$

$$\Longleftrightarrow q^u \quad \leq \frac{2}{5}$$

and (nonbinding condition)

$$\frac{6 - 15 \cdot q^u}{5} \leq 1$$

$$\Longleftrightarrow q^u \quad \geq \frac{1}{15}$$

as well as (binding condition)

$$q^d = 1 - q^u - q^m \geq 0$$

$$\Longleftrightarrow q^u \quad \geq \frac{1}{10}$$

and (nonbinding condition)

$$q^d = 1 - q^u - q^m \leq 1$$

$$\Longleftrightarrow q^u \quad \leq \frac{3}{5}$$

Therefore, there are infinitely many probability measures that make the discounted stock price process a martingale. Setting $q \equiv q^u$, the set of all martingale measures $\mathbb{Q}$ consistent with the market model is:

$$\mathbb{Q} = \left\{ \left(\begin{array}{c} q \\ \dfrac{6 - 15 \cdot q}{5} \\ 1 - q - \dfrac{6 - 15 \cdot q}{5} \end{array} \right), \frac{1}{10} \leq q \leq \frac{2}{5} \right\}$$

As an example, take $q = \frac{3}{10}$. It follows

$$Q\left(q = \frac{3}{10}\right) = \left(\begin{array}{c} \dfrac{3}{10} \\ \dfrac{6 - 15 \cdot \frac{3}{10}}{5} \\ 1 - \dfrac{3}{10} - \dfrac{3}{10} \end{array} \right) = \left(\begin{array}{c} \dfrac{3}{10} \\ \dfrac{3}{10} \\ \dfrac{4}{10} \end{array} \right)$$

and

$$\frac{3}{10} \cdot 20 + \frac{3}{10} \cdot 10 + \frac{4}{10} \cdot 5 = 11$$

as desired for the stock price process.

With the specifications from before, the calculation in Python is as follows:

```
In [14]: Q = np.array((0.3, 0.3, 0.4))
```

```
In [15]: np.dot(Q, S[1])
Out[15]: 11.0
```

According to the 2FTAP, the market model is *incomplete* since there is more than one martingale measure consistent with the market model.

Martingale Measures in Incomplete Markets

Complete market models are characterized by a unique martingale measure. By contrast, incomplete market models usually allow for an infinite number of martingale measures consistent with the model economy. It should be clear that this has significant consequences for the pricing of contingent claims since different martingale measures will lead to different values of contingent claims that are all consistent with the absence of arbitrage.

Risk-Neutral Pricing

What implications does an infinite number of market consistent martingale measures have when it comes to the arbitrage pricing of contingent claims? First, for those contingent claims that are attainable, $\mathbb{A}$, arbitrage pricing holds as in a complete market setting: the value of the replicating portfolio equals the price of the contingent claim to be replicated—otherwise arbitrage opportunities exist. Formally, $C_0 = V_0(\phi)$ if $V_1(\phi) = C_1$.

For those contingent claims that are not attainable, $C_1 \in \overline{\mathbb{A}} = \mathbb{R}^3 \setminus \mathbb{A}$, the answer is not that simple. Suppose the first Arrow-Debreu security γ^u. It is not replicable as shown previously and therefore belongs to the set $\overline{\mathbb{A}}$. Its martingale price is:

$$\gamma_0^u(q) = \frac{1}{1+i} \cdot \mathbb{E}^Q\left((1,0,0)^T\right) = \frac{1}{1+i} \cdot q$$

The quantity γ_0^ω is often called the *state price* for one unit of currency in state $\omega \in \Omega$. It is simply the discounted martingale probability for this state.

In the model economy, $\frac{1}{10} \leq q \leq \frac{2}{5}$ must hold, therefore the martingale price—the price avoiding arbitrage opportunities—lies in the interval:

$$\frac{10}{11} \cdot \frac{1}{10} = \frac{1}{11} \leq \gamma_0^u \leq \frac{10}{11} \cdot \frac{2}{5} = \frac{4}{11}$$

In words, every price between $\frac{1}{11}$ and $\frac{4}{11}$ for the first Arrow-Debreu security is consistent with the absence of arbitrage, given the assumptions for the model economy. Calculations for other contingent claims that are not attainable lead to similar results.

Super-Replication

Replication is important not only in a *pricing* context. It is also an approach to *hedge risk* resulting from an uncertain contingent claim payoff. Consider an arbitrary attainable contingent claim. Selling short the replication portfolio in addition to holding the contingent claim eliminates any kind of risk resulting from uncertainty regarding future payoff. This is because the payoffs of the contingent claim and the replicating portfolio cancel each other out perfectly. Formally, if the portfolio ϕ^* replicates contingent claim C_1, then:

$$C_1 - V_1(\phi^*) = C_1 - \mathcal{M} \cdot \phi^* = 0$$

For a contingent claim that is not attainable, such a perfect hedge is not available. However, one can always compose a portfolio that *super-replicates* the payoff of such a contingent claim. A portfolio ϕ super-replicates a contingent claim C_1 if its payoff in every future state of the economy is greater than or equal to the contingent claims payoff $V_1(\phi) \geq C_1$.

Consider again the first Arrow-Debreu security γ^u, which is not attainable. The payoff can be super-replicated, for example, by a portfolio containing the risk-less bond only:

$$\phi = \left(\frac{1}{B_1}, 0\right)^T$$

The resulting payoff is

$$V_1(\phi) = \frac{1}{B_1} \cdot \begin{pmatrix} B_1 \\ B_1 \\ B_1 \end{pmatrix} = \begin{pmatrix} 1 \\ 1 \\ 1 \end{pmatrix} \geq \begin{pmatrix} 1 \\ 0 \\ 0 \end{pmatrix} = C_1$$

where the $\geq$ sign is to be understood element-wise. Although this satisfies the definition of super-replication, it might not be the best choice in terms of the costs to set up the super-replication portfolio. Therefore, a *cost minimization* argument is introduced in general.

The *super-replication problem* for a contingent claim C_1 at *minimal costs* is:

$$\min_{\phi} V_0(\phi)$$
$$\text{s.t. } V_1(\phi) \geq C_1$$

or

$$\min_{b,s} b \cdot B_0 + s \cdot S_0$$
$$\text{s.t. } \begin{cases} b \cdot B_1 + s \cdot S_1^u \geq C_1^u \\ b \cdot B_1 + s \cdot S_1^m \geq C_1^m \\ b \cdot B_1 + s \cdot S_1^d \geq C_1^d \end{cases}$$

Such minimization problems can be modeled and solved straightforwardly in Python when using the SciPy (*http://scipy.org*) package. The following code starts by calculating the costs for the inefficient super-replication portfolio using the bond only. It proceeds by defining a value function for a portfolio. It also illustrates that alternative portfolio compositions can indeed be more cost efficient:

```
In [16]: C1 = np.array((1, 0, 0))   ❶

In [17]: 1 / B[1][0] * B[1] >= C1   ❷
Out[17]: array([ True,   True,   True])

In [18]: 1 / B[1][0] * B[0]   ❸
Out[18]: 0.9090909090909092

In [19]: def V(phi, t):   ❹
             return phi[0] * B[t] + phi[1] * S[t]

In [20]: phi = np.array((0.04, 0.03))   ❺

In [21]: V(phi, 0)   ❻
Out[21]: 0.7

In [22]: V(phi, 1)   ❼
Out[22]: array([1.04, 0.74, 0.59])
```

❶ The payoff of the contingent claim (first Arrow-Debreu security).

❷ The portfolio with the bond only checked for the super-replication characteristic.

❸ The costs to set up this portfolio.

❹ A function to calculate the value of a portfolio phi today, t=0, or in one year, t=1.

❺ Another guess for a super-replicating portfolio.

❻ The cost to set it up, which is lower than with the bond only.

❼ And the resulting value (payoff) in one year, which super-replicates the first Arrow-Debreu security.

The second part of the code implements the *minimization program* based on the previous inequality constraints in vectorized fashion. The cost optimal super-replication portfolio is much cheaper than the one using the bond only or the already more efficient portfolio including the bond and the stock:

```
In [23]: from scipy.optimize import minimize   ❶

In [24]: cons = ({'type': 'ineq', 'fun': lambda phi: V(phi, 1) - C1})   ❷
```

```
In [25]: res = minimize(lambda phi: V(phi, 0),   ❸
                        (0.01, 0.01),   ❹
                        method='SLSQP',   ❺
                        constraints=cons)   ❻

In [26]: res   ❼
Out[26]:     fun: 0.3636363636310989
             jac: array([10., 10.])
         message: 'Optimization terminated successfully'
            nfev: 6
             nit: 2
            njev: 2
          status: 0
         success: True
               x: array([-0.0303 ,  0.06667])

In [27]: V(res['x'], 0)   ❽
Out[27]: 0.3636363636310989

In [28]: V(res['x'], 1)   ❾
Out[28]: array([ 1.    ,  0.33333, -0.    ])
```

❶ Imports the `minimize` function from `scipy.optimize`.

❷ Defines the inequality constraints in vectorized fashion based on a `lambda` (or anonymous) function; the function λ modeled here is $\lambda(\phi) = V_1(\phi) - C_1$, for which the inequality constraint $\lambda(\phi) \geq 0$ must hold.

❸ The function to be minimized also as a `lambda` function.

❹ An initial guess for the optimal solution (not too important here).

❺ The method to be used for the minimization, here Sequential Least Squares Programming (SLSQP).

❻ The constraints for the minimization problem as defined before.

❼ The complete results dictionary from the minimization, with the optimal parameters under x and the minimal function value under `fun`.

❽ The value of the optimal super-replicating portfolio today.

❾ The future uncertain value of the optimal super-replicating portfolio; the optimal portfolio that sells short the bond and goes long the stock exactly replicates the relevant payoff in two states and only super-replicates in the middle state.

Approximate Replication

Super-replication assumes a somewhat extreme situation: the payoff of the contingent claim to be super-replicated must be reached or exceeded in any given state under any circumstances. Such a situation is seen in practice, for instance, when a life insurance company invests in a way that it can meet under all circumstances—which often translates in the real world into something like "With a probability of 99.9%."—its future liabilities and obligations (contingent claims). However, this might not be an economically sensible or even viable option in many cases.

This is where *approximation* comes into play. The idea is to replicate the payoff of a contingent claim *as well as possible* given an objective function. The problem then becomes minimizing the *replication error* given the traded financial assets.

A possible candidate for the objective or error function is the *mean squared error* (MSE). Let $V_1(\phi)$ be the value vector given a replication portfolio ϕ. The MSE for a contingent claim C_1 given the portfolio ϕ is:

$$MSE\big(V_1(\phi) - C_1\big) = \frac{1}{|\Omega|} \sum_{\omega \in \Omega} \big(V_1^{\omega}(\phi) - C_1^{\omega}\big)^2$$

This is the quantity to be minimized. For an attainable contingent claim, the MSE is zero. The problem itself in matrix form is:

$$\min_{\phi} MSE\big(\mathcal{M} \cdot \phi - C_1\big)$$

In linear algebra, this is a problem that falls in the category of *ordinary least-squares regression* (OLS regression) problems. The previous problem is the special case of a *linear* OLS regression problem.

NumPy provides the function `np.linalg.lstsq` that solves problems of this kind in a standardized and efficient manner:

```
In [29]: M = np.array((B[1], S[1])).T   ❶

In [30]: M   ❶
Out[30]: array([[11, 20],
                [11, 10],
                [11,  5]])

In [31]: reg = np.linalg.lstsq(M, C1, rcond=-1)   ❷

In [32]: reg
         # (array,    ❸
         #  array,    ❹
         #  int,      ❺
```

```
            #  array)  ❻
Out[32]: (array([-0.04545,  0.07143]), array([0.07143]), 2, array([28.93836,
            7.11136]))

In [33]: V(reg[0], 0)  ❼
Out[33]: 0.2597402597402598

In [34]: V(reg[0], 1)  ❽
Out[34]: array([ 0.92857,  0.21429, -0.14286])

In [35]: V(reg[0], 1) - C1  ❾
Out[35]: array([-0.07143,  0.21429, -0.14286])

In [36]: np.mean((V(reg[0], 1) - C1) ** 2)  ❿
Out[36]: 0.02380952380952381
```

❶ The future price matrix of the two traded financial assets.

❷ This solves the linear OLS regression problem by minimizing the MSE.

❸ The optimal portfolio positions, that is, the solution to the problem.

❹ The MSE obtained from the optimization procedure (minimal mean squared replication error).

❺ Rank of matrix M…

❻ …and its singular values.

❼ The value of the approximate portfolio (lower than the value of the cost-minimizing portfolio).

❽ The payoff of the approximation portfolio.

❾ The vector with the replication errors.

❿ The MSE from the approximate replication.

Approximate replication might not be applicable in all circumstances. But an investor or financial manager with discretion in their decisions can decide that an approximation is simply good enough. Such a decision could be made, for example, in cases in which super-replication might be considered to be too costly.

Capital Market Line

Assume a mean-variance or, rather, mean-volatility context. In what follows, the risky stock is interpreted as the *market portfolio*. One can think of the market portfolio in terms of a broad stock index—in the spirit of the S&P 500 stock index.

As before, agents can compose portfolios that consist of the bond and the market portfolio. The rate of return for the bond—the risk-less interest rate—is $i = 0.1$, and the volatility is 0. The expected rate of return for the market portfolio is:

$$\mu_S = \frac{\mathbf{E}^P(S_1)}{S_0} - 1 = \frac{7}{6} - 1 = \frac{1}{6}$$

Its volatility is:

$$\sigma_S = \sqrt{\mathbf{E}^P\left(\left(\frac{S_1 - S_0}{S_0} - \mu_S\right)^2\right)}$$

Quick calculations in Python give the corresponding numerical values:

```
In [37]: mu_S = 7 / 6 - 1    ❶

In [38]: mu_S    ❶
Out[38]: 0.16666666666666674

In [39]: sigma_S = (S[1] / S[0]).std()    ❷

In [40]: sigma_S    ❷
Out[40]: 0.6236095644623235
```

❶ The expected return of the market portfolio.

❷ The volatility of the returns of the market portfolio.[1]

Feasible mean values for a normalized portfolio with total weight of 1 or 100% consisting of the bond and the market portfolio without short selling range from 0 to about 0.166. Regarding the volatility, values between 0 and about 0.623 are possible.

---

1 Note that this calculation for the volatility is only valid since an equal probability is assumed for the three states.

Allowing for short selling, Figure 3-2 shows the *capital market line* (CML) resulting from different portfolio compositions. Because short selling of the bond is allowed, risk-return combinations on the upper line (with positive slope) are possible, which is what is referred to in general as *the* CML. The lower line (with negative slope) is in principle irrelevant since such portfolios, resulting from short positions in the market portfolio, have lower expected rates of return at the same risk as those that have a corresponding long position in the market portfolio:

```
In [41]: s = np.linspace(-2, 2, 25)  ❶

In [42]: b = (1 - s)  ❷

In [43]: i = 0.1  ❸

In [44]: mu = b * i + s * mu_S  ❹

In [45]: sigma = np.abs(s * sigma_S)  ❺

In [46]: plt.figure(figsize=(10, 6))
         plt.plot(sigma, mu)  ❻
         plt.xlabel('$\sigma$')
         plt.ylabel('$\mu$');
```

❶ The market portfolio position takes on values between −200% and 200%.

❷ The bond portfolio position fills up to 100% total portfolio weight.

❸ The risk-less interest rate.

❹ The resulting expected rates of return for the portfolio.

❺ The resulting volatility values for the portfolio.

❻ Plots the CML for short as well as long positions in the market portfolio.

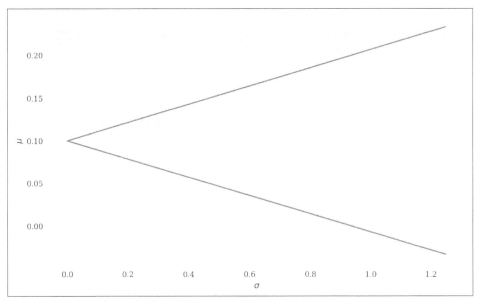

Figure 3-2. Capital market line (upper, increasing part)

The equation describing the (upper, increasing part of the) CML is:

$$\mu = i + \frac{\mu_S - i}{\sigma_S} \cdot \sigma$$

Capital Asset Pricing Model

The *Capital Asset Pricing Model* (CAPM) as pioneered by Sharpe (1964) is an equilibrium pricing model that mainly relates the expected rate of return of an arbitrary financial asset or portfolio and its volatility with the market portfolio's expected rate of return and volatility.

To this end, the *correlation* between the rates of return of a financial asset and the market portfolio is of importance. In addition to the market portfolio, consider another risky financial asset with price process $T = (T_0, T_1)$. The correlation ρ is defined by:

$$\rho_{ST} = \frac{\mathbf{E}^P\left(\left(r_1^S - \mu_S\right) \cdot \left(r_1^T - \mu_T\right)\right)}{\sigma_S \cdot \sigma_T}$$

with $-1 \leq \rho_{ST} \leq 1$. If the correlation is positive, the two financial assets have a tendency to move in the same direction. If it is negative, the financial assets have a tendency to move in opposite directions. In the special case of perfect positive correlation, $\rho_{ST} = 1$, the two financial assets always move in the same direction. This is true, for instance, for portfolios that lie on the CML for which the rates of return are just the rates of return of the market portfolio scaled by the weight of the market portfolio. Uncertainty in this case arises from the market portfolio part only such that any variation in risk is due to the market portfolio weight variation.

Consider the case of a financial asset T, which is part of the market portfolio and for which the correlation with the market portfolio shall not be perfect. For such a financial asset, the expected rate of return is given by:

$$\mu_T = i + \frac{(\mu_S - i) \cdot \rho_{ST}}{\sigma_S} \cdot \sigma_T$$

$$= i + \frac{\rho_{ST} \cdot \sigma_S \cdot \sigma_T}{\sigma_S^2} \cdot (\mu_S - i)$$

It is easy to verify that the correlation between the market portfolio and the bond is zero such that the previous relationship gives the risk-less interest as the expected return if the financial asset T is the risk-less bond.

The *covariance* between S_1 and T_1 is defined as $\sigma_{ST} = \rho_{ST} \cdot \sigma_S \cdot \sigma_T$ such that

$$\mu_T = i + \frac{\sigma_{ST}}{\sigma_S^2} \cdot (\mu_S - i)$$

$$= i + \beta_T \cdot (\mu_S - i)$$

with

$$\beta_T \equiv \frac{\sigma_{ST}}{\sigma_S^2}$$

This gives the famous CAPM linear relationship between the expected rate of return of the market portfolio and the expected return of the financial asset T—or any other financial asset to this end. In that sense, the CAPM states that the rate of return for any financial asset is only determined by the expected excess return of the market portfolio over the risk-less interest rate and the beta factor, which is the covariance between the two, scaled by the square of the market portfolio volatility (variance of returns).

For the CAPM, the CML is replaced by the *security market line* (SML), which is plotted in beta-return space as follows. A visualization is given in Figure 3-3:

```
In [47]: beta = np.linspace(0, 2, 25)  ❶

In [48]: mu = i + beta * (mu_S - i)  ❷

In [49]: plt.figure(figsize=(10, 6))
         plt.plot(beta, mu, label='security market line')  ❸
         plt.xlabel('$\\beta$')
         plt.ylabel('$\mu$')
         plt.ylim(0, 0.25)  ❹
         plt.plot(1, mu_S, 'ro', label='market portfolio')  ❺
         plt.legend(loc=0);
```

❶ Generates an ndarray object with the beta values.

❷ Calculates the expected returns mu according to the CAPM.

❸ Plots the beta-mu combinations.

❹ Adjusts the limits for the y axis.

❺ Plots the beta and expected return of the market portfolio.

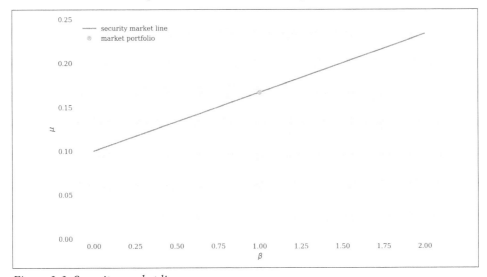

Figure 3-3. Security market line

But why do the preceding relationships—and in particular the CAPM formula—hold true in the first place? To answer this question, consider a portfolio with normalized weight of 1 or 100% of which a proportion a is invested in financial asset T and the remainder $1 - a$ is invested in the market portfolio. The expected rate of return of this portfolio is:

$$\mu(a) = a \cdot \mu_T + (1 - a) \cdot \mu_S$$

The volatility of the portfolio is (see Sharpe (1964)):

$$\sigma(a) = \left(a^2 \cdot \sigma_T^2 + (1 - a)^2 \cdot \sigma_S^2 + 2 \cdot a \cdot (1 - a) \cdot \sigma_{ST} \right)^{\frac{1}{2}}$$

The marginal change in the expected portfolio rate of return, given a marginal change in the allocation of the financial asset T, is determined by the following partial derivative:

$$\frac{\partial \mu}{\partial a} = \mu_T - \mu_S$$

The marginal change in the portfolio volatility, given a marginal change in the allocation of the financial asset T, is determined by the following partial derivative:

$$\frac{\partial \sigma}{\partial a} = \frac{a \cdot \sigma_T^2 - \sigma_S^2 + a \cdot \sigma_S^2 + \sigma_{ST} - 2 \cdot a \cdot \sigma_{ST}}{\sqrt{a^2 \cdot \sigma_T^2 + (1 - a)^2 \cdot \sigma_S^2 + 2 \cdot a \cdot (1 - a) \cdot \sigma_{ST}}}$$

The basic insight of the CAPM as an *equilibrium model* is that the financial asset T is already part of the market portfolio. Therefore, a can only be interpreted as the *excess demand* for the financial asset, and in equilibrium when excess demand for all financial assets *is zero*, a also must equal zero. Therefore, in equilibrium, the partial derivative for the expected portfolio rate of return remains unchanged, while the one for the portfolio volatility simplifies significantly when evaluated at the equilibrium point $a = 0$:

$$\left. \frac{\partial \sigma}{\partial a} \right|_{a = 0} = \frac{1}{2} \sigma_S \cdot \left(-2 \cdot \sigma_S^2 + 2 \cdot \sigma_{ST} \right)$$

$$= \sigma_S \cdot \sigma_{ST} - \sigma_S \cdot \sigma_S^2$$

$$= \frac{\sigma_{ST} - \sigma_S^2}{\sigma_S}$$

The *risk-return trade-off* in market equilibrium therefore is:

$$
\left. \frac{\frac{\partial \mu}{\partial a}}{\frac{\partial \sigma}{\partial a}} \right|_{a=0} = \frac{\mu_T - \mu_S}{\frac{\sigma_{ST} - \sigma_S^2}{\sigma_S}}
$$

The final insight needed to derive the preceding *CAPM formula* is that in equilibrium, the previous term needs to be equal to the slope of the CML:

$$
\frac{\mu_T - \mu_S}{\frac{\sigma_{ST} - \sigma_S^2}{\sigma_S}} = \frac{\mu_S - i}{\sigma_S}
$$

$$
\Longleftrightarrow \mu_T = i + \frac{\sigma_{ST}}{\sigma_S^2} \cdot (\mu_S - i)
$$

$$
= i + \beta_T \cdot (\mu_S - i)
$$

How does the CAPM help in pricing a financial asset that is not replicable? Given the vector of uncertain prices in one year of a financial asset T_1, the uncertain rates of return are

$$
r^T = \frac{T_1 - T_0}{T_0}
$$

where T_0 is the equilibrium price today to be determined. The following relationship holds as well:

$$
\mu_T = \frac{\mathbf{E}^P(T_1) - T_0}{T_0}
$$

Define now the *unit price of risk* as the excess return of the market portfolio per unit of variance by

$$
\lambda = \frac{\mu_S - i}{\sigma_S^2}
$$

such that according to the CAPM, one gets

$$\mu_T = i + \lambda \cdot \sigma_{ST}$$

This shows that in equilibrium the expected rate of return of a financial asset is determined only by its covariance with the market portfolio. Equating this with the preceding term for the expected return of the financial asset T yields

$$\frac{\mathbf{E}^P(T_1) - T_0}{T_0} = i + \lambda \cdot \sigma_{ST}$$

$$\Leftrightarrow T_0 = \frac{\mathbf{E}^P(T_1)}{1 + i + \lambda \cdot \sigma_{ST}}$$

The denominator can be thought of as a *risk-adjusted discount factor*.

MVP, CAPM, and Market Completeness

Both MVP and the CAPM rely on high-level statistics only, such as expectation, volatility, and covariance. When replicating contingent claims, for example, every single payoff in every possible future state plays an important role—with the demonstrated consequences resulting from market incompleteness. In MVP and CAPM contexts, it is (implicitly) assumed that investors only care about aggregate statistics and not really about every single state.

Consider the example of two financial assets with the same initial prices under an equal probability measure, one paying 20 currency units in one state and nothing in the others, and the other one paying 20 currency units in a different state as the other financial asset and nothing else. Both financial assets have the same risk-return characteristics. However, an agent might strongly prefer one over the other—independent of the fact that their aggregate statistics are the same. Focusing on risk and return is often a convenient simplification but not always an appropriate one.

Conclusions

The major topic of this chapter is incomplete financial markets. Moving from a two-state model economy to one with three states and keeping the number of traded financial assets constant at two, immediately results in market incompleteness. This in turn implies that contingent claims are in general not perfectly replicable by portfolios composed of the risk-less bond and the risky stock.

However, payoffs of contingent claims can be super-replicated if they must be met or surpassed under all circumstances. While there are in general infinitely many such super-replication portfolios, it is generally required that the cost-minimizing portfolio be chosen. If there is a bit more flexibility, the payoffs of contingent claims that are not attainable can also be approximated. In this context, the replication problem is replaced by an optimization problem, according to which the mean squared error of the replication portfolio is minimized. Mathematically, this boils down to a linear OLS regression problem.

The CAPM is based on equilibrium pricing arguments to derive expected rates of return and also prices for traded financial assets given their risk-return characteristics in the mean-volatility space. A central role is played by the correlation and the covariance of a financial asset with the market portfolio, which is assumed to contain the financial asset itself.

Further Resources

Articles and books cited in this chapter:

Pliska, Stanley. 1997. *Introduction to Mathematical Finance*. Malden and Oxford: Blackwell Publishers.

Sharpe, William. 1964. "Capital Asset Prices: A Theory of Market Equilibrium under Conditions of Risk." *The Journal of Finance* 19 (3): 425–442.

## CHAPTER 4

Optimality and Equilibrium

Much of economic theory is based on the premise: given two alternatives, an agent can, and will if able, choose a preferred one.

—Darrell Duffie (1988)

A portfolio analysis starts with information concerning individual securities. It ends with conclusions concerning portfolios as a whole. The purpose of the analysis is to find portfolios which best meet the objectives of the investor.

—Harry Markowitz (1959)

This chapter is about the modeling of agents and their optimization problems. It presents some of the fundamental building blocks of microeconomic theory (see Varian (1992)) and financial economics (see Eichberger and Harper (1997)). At the core of this chapter is the *expected utility maximization* paradigm, which is the dominant way of modeling an agent's preferences in financial economics. Based on this paradigm, two central topics are discussed.

First, we discuss how an agent chooses an optimal investment portfolio given their preferences and the initial wealth. This type of problem is typically called *optimal portfolio choice*. The approach presented here does not rely on any form of simplification as seen with the mean-variance portfolio (MVP) approach and the Capital Asset Pricing Model (CAPM) that, for example, reduce the problem of choosing investment portfolios to the first and second moments of the return distributions of financial assets as well as their covariance.

Second, while prices for financial assets in the previous two chapters have been given a priori, this chapter derives them from fundamental principles in that it analyzes the *pricing of financial assets* based on the optimization problem of a so-called *representative agent* in addition to *equilibrium arguments*. Loosely speaking, a representative agent can be thought of as the aggregation of (infinitely) many agents acting independently in (financial) markets. Conditions for the existence of such a representative agent are well-known (see chapter 6 in Milne (1995))—however, they are not discussed in this chapter because financial theory in general simply postulates the existence.

The current chapter mainly covers the following topics from finance, mathematics, and Python programming. On the Python side, not that many new elements are introduced. The basic mathematical and Python tool sets for doing finance in discrete models are already introduced and developed in the previous two chapters:

Finance	Mathematics	Python
Preferences and utility	Utility function	NumPy
Utility maximization	Objective function, budget constraint, Theorem of Lagrange	scipy.optimize.minimize
Indifference curves, budget line	Function	NumPy, matplotlib
Logarithmic utility	Natural logarithm	NumPy, matplotlib
Time-additive utility	Utility function	NumPy, scipy.optimize.minimize
(time-additive) expected utility	Probability measure, Theorem of Lagrange	NumPy, scipy.optimize.minimize
Optimal investment portfolio	Theorem of Lagrange, first-order conditions	NumPy, scipy.optimize.minimize
Equilibrium pricing, representative agent	Theorem of Lagrange, first-order conditions	NumPy, scipy.optimize.minimize, SymPy
Martingale measures in incomplete markets	Set of probability measures	SymPy, sy.Symbol, sy.solve
Market completion by contingent claims	Theorem of Lagrange, first-order conditions	NumPy, scipy.optimize.minimize

Utility Maximization

Formally, an agent is modeled by a *utility function*, which orders a set of choices the agent is faced with and which is a representation of the agent's *preferences* (see chapter 7 in Varian (1992)). Consider the static economy without uncertainty from Chapter 2. In addition, assume that an agent is endowed with some initial wealth, $w \in \mathbb{R}_{>0}$. The agent can decide how much of this wealth to spend today, $t = 0$, and how much to save—via bank deposits—for future consumption. One can think of an agent faced with the question of how much to save for retirement.

The agent receives utility from money today, c_0, and in one year, c_1, according to the utility function:

$$U: \mathbb{R}_{\geq 0}^2 \to \mathbb{R}_{\geq 0}, \left(c_0, c_1\right) \mapsto u\left(c_0, c_1\right)$$

As an example, assume $u(c_0, c_1) = c_0 \cdot c_1$—expressing the idea that money today and in one year are substitutes, although not perfect ones (if either one is zero, utility is zero as well). What is the optimal consumption-saving plan for the agent? Their constrained optimization problem formally is:

$$\max_{c_0, c_1} c_0 \cdot c_1$$
$$\text{s.t. } c_0 + c_1 = w$$

According to the Theorem of Lagrange (see chapter 5 in Sundaram (1996)), the constrained optimization problem can be transformed into an unconstrained one of the form:

$$\max_{c_0, c_1, \lambda} f(c_0, c_1, \lambda) = c_0 \cdot c_1 - \lambda \cdot (c_0 + c_1 - w)$$

The first-order necessary conditions for optimality are:

$$\begin{cases} \dfrac{\partial f}{\partial c_0} &= \quad c_1 - \lambda = 0 \\[2mm] \dfrac{\partial f}{\partial c_1} &= \quad c_0 - \lambda = 0 \\[2mm] \dfrac{\partial f}{\partial \lambda} &= \quad c_0 + c_1 - w = 0 \end{cases}$$

From these, one easily derives $c_0 = c_1 = \frac{w}{2}$ as the optimal consumption-saving plan.

This optimization problem can be modeled and solved in Python numerically, for which $w = 10$ shall hold:

```
In [1]: def u(c):
            return -c[0] * c[1]    ❶

In [2]: w = 10    ❷

In [3]: from scipy.optimize import minimize

In [4]: cons = ({'type': 'eq', 'fun': lambda c: c[0] + c[1] - w})    ❸

In [5]: opt = minimize(u, (1, 1), constraints=cons)    ❹

In [6]: opt
Out[6]:     fun: -24.999999999999996
            jac: array([-5., -5.])
        message: 'Optimization terminated successfully'
```

```
            nfev: 6
             nit: 2
            njev: 2
          status: 0
         success: True
               x: array([5., 5.])

In [7]: opt['x']   ❺
Out[7]: array([5., 5.])

In [8]: -opt['fun']   ❻
Out[8]: 24.999999999999996
```

❶ The utility function with a negative sign to accomplish a maximization through minimization.

❷ The initial wealth of the agent to be distributed between today and the future.

❸ The budget constraint as an equality constraint for the `minimize` function.

❹ The optimization with initial guess and budget constraint.

❺ The optimal consumption-saving plan.

❻ The maximum utility gained through the optimal plan.

Indifference Curves

The optimal solution from the previous section can be visualized by the means of *indifference curves*. An indifference curve is formed by all such combinations $c = (c_0, c_1)$ that give the same utility $\bar{u}$. The equation describing such a curve in (c_0, c_1) space is:

$$\bar{u} = c_0 \cdot c_1$$

$$\Longleftrightarrow c_1 = \frac{\bar{u}}{c_0}$$

The equation describing the line representing the *budget constraint* is:

$$w = c_0 + c_1$$

$$\Longleftrightarrow c_1 = w - c_0$$

The optimization problem is visualized in Figure 4-1, where the optimal plan is given by the dot—this is where the indifference curve for $\bar{u} = 25$ is tangent to the line representing the budget constraint.

In Python, this translates into the following code:

```
In [9]: def iu(u, c0):
            return u / c0      ❶

In [10]: def c1(c0):
             return w - c0     ❷

In [11]: import numpy as np
         np.set_printoptions(precision=5)

In [12]: from pylab import mpl, plt
         plt.style.use('seaborn')
         mpl.rcParams['savefig.dpi'] = 300
         mpl.rcParams['font.family'] = 'serif'

In [13]: c0 = np.linspace(1, w)      ❸

In [14]: plt.figure(figsize=(10, 6))
         plt.plot(c0, c1(c0), label='budget constraint', lw=3.0)
         plt.plot(c0, iu(15, c0), '--', label='$u=15$')
         plt.plot(c0, iu(25, c0), label='$u=25$')
         plt.plot(c0, iu(35, c0), '-.', label='$u=35$')
         plt.plot(opt['x'][0], opt['x'][1], 'ro', label='$c=(5, 5)$')
         plt.legend(loc=0);
```

❶ Function for indifference curve.

❷ Function for budget line.

❸ The domain over which to plot both.

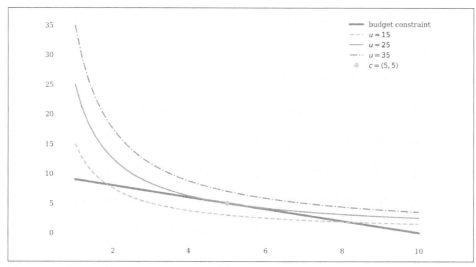

Figure 4-1. The utility maximization problem

Appropriate Utility Functions

In finance, the utility that an agent gains from money they have available at a certain point in time—as a substitute for any other real asset that might be bought with the money, for instance—is typically expressed as a function $u: \mathbb{R}_{\geq 0} \to \mathbb{R}$, which is assumed to satisfy three conditions:

1. $u(x)$ is twice differentiable

2. $\frac{du}{dx} > 0$

3. $\frac{d^2u}{dx^2} \leq 0$

The first condition is a technical prerequisite for the other two. The second condition formalizes the idea that more money—everything else being equal—is better than less money. Agents are assumed to be insatiable. The third condition states that the marginal utility from an additional unit of money is smaller (or the same at the maximum) than the marginal utility of the previous marginal unit of money. The function is therewith assumed to be increasing and (quasi-)concave.

Logarithmic Utility

This section introduces a type of function that is well suited for financial analyses based on a utility maximizing agent. Such a function—that satisfies the three conditions of the previous section and that is regularly used in finance to model the utility an agent receives from money (or consumption)—is the *natural logarithm* $u(x) = \ln x$. For it, one gets:

1. $\frac{du}{dx} = \frac{1}{x} > 0$ for $x \in \mathbb{R}_{>0}$

2. $\frac{d^2u}{dx^2} = -\frac{1}{x^2} < 0$ for $x \in \mathbb{R}_{>0}$

Python allows us to visualize the three relevant functions. NumPy is used in combination with vectorized calculations. Figure 4-2 shows the plot as generated by the following code:

```
In [15]: x = np.linspace(0.5, 10, 50)    ❶

In [16]: x[:5]    ❷
Out[16]: array([0.5     , 0.69388, 0.88776, 1.08163, 1.27551])

In [17]: u = np.log(x)    ❸

In [18]: u1 = 1 / x    ❹

In [19]: u2 = -1 / x ** 2    ❺

In [20]: plt.figure(figsize=(10, 6))    ❻
         plt.plot(x, u, label='$u$')    ❼
         plt.plot(x, u1, '--', label='$du/dx$')    ❽
         plt.plot(x, u2, '-.', label='$d^2u/dx^2$')    ❾
         plt.legend(loc=0);    ❿
```

❶ Creates an ndarray object with floating point numbers between 0.5 and 10 and a homogeneous spacing to get 50 values.

❷ Shows a selection of the resulting numbers.

❸ Calculates the values for the utility function.

❹ And for its first derivative as well as…

❺ …for its second derivative.

❻ Creates a new canvas for plotting and provides sizing parameters.

❼ Plots the utility function.

❽ Plots the first derivative.

❾ Plots the second derivative.

❿ Puts a legend in the optimal location (`loc=0`).

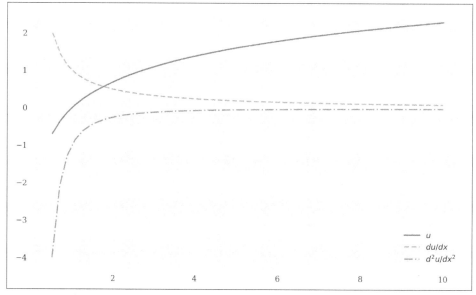

Figure 4-2. The natural logarithm function and its first and second derivatives

Time-Additive Utility

Using the natural logarithm as a function to model utility of an agent from money, the preferences of an agent over consumption-saving plans $c = (c_0, c_1)$ can be described as a time-additive function of the following form:

$$U : \mathbb{R}^2_{\geq 0} \to \mathbb{R}, (c_0, c_1) \mapsto \ln c_0 + \kappa \cdot \ln c_1$$

$\kappa \in \mathbb{R}_{\geq 0}$ is assumed to take on values $0 < \kappa \leq 1$ and represents the *time preference* of the agent. It embodies the idea that money and consumption today are valued higher than in one year. At least weakly, 100 USD now is preferred to 100 USD in one year— no matter what exact function describes utility (assuming consistency of preferences over time). It can be thought of as a nonmonetary discount factor. It is easily verified that this function satisfies the three conditions described previously—it is twice differentiable, increasing, and concave—based on the partial derivatives with regard to both c_0 and c_1.

If the agent has initial wealth of w, their constrained optimization problem is:

$$\max_{c_0, c_1} \ln c_0 + \kappa \cdot \ln c_1$$

$$\text{s.t. } c_0 + c_1 = w$$

or

$$\max_{c_0, c_1, \lambda} f(c_0, c_1, \lambda) = \ln c_0 + \kappa \cdot \ln c_1 - \lambda \cdot (c_0 + c_1 - w)$$

The first-order necessary conditions for optimality are:

$$\begin{cases} \dfrac{\partial f}{\partial c_0} &= \dfrac{1}{c_0} - \lambda = 0 \\[2mm] \dfrac{\partial f}{\partial c_1} &= \kappa \cdot \dfrac{1}{c_1} - \lambda = 0 \\[2mm] \dfrac{\partial f}{\partial \lambda} &= c_0 + c_1 - w = 0 \end{cases}$$

From these, one obtains:

$$\frac{1}{c_0} = \kappa \cdot \frac{1}{c_1}$$

$$\Longleftrightarrow c_1 = \kappa \cdot c_0$$

The optimal consumption-saving plan now reflects the time preference in that consumption in one year c_1 is set to $\kappa \cdot c_0$. It also holds

$$c_0 + \kappa \cdot c_0 = w$$

$$\Longleftrightarrow c_0 = \frac{w}{1 + \kappa}$$

and

$$\frac{w}{1 + \kappa} + c_1 = w$$

$$\iff c_1 = \frac{\kappa \cdot w}{1 + \kappa}$$

The budget constraint is binding:

$$\frac{w}{1 + \kappa} + \frac{\kappa \cdot w}{1 + \kappa} = \frac{w + \kappa \cdot w}{1 + \kappa} = w$$

The following code solves the optimization problem numerically for $w = 10$. The optimal plan reflects the time preference:

```
In [21]: import math

In [22]: from scipy.optimize import minimize

In [23]: kappa = 10 / 11

In [24]: def U(c):
             return -(math.log(c[0]) +  kappa * math.log(c[1]))   ❶

In [25]: w = 10

In [26]: cons = ({'type': 'eq', 'fun': lambda c: c[0] + c[1] - w})   ❷

In [27]: opt = minimize(U, (1, 1), constraints=cons)

In [28]: opt
Out[28]:      fun: -3.0747286083026886
              jac: array([-0.19091, -0.19091])
          message: 'Optimization terminated successfully'
             nfev: 18
              nit: 6
             njev: 6
           status: 0
          success: True
                x: array([5.23811, 4.76189])

In [29]: opt['x']   ❸
Out[29]: array([5.23811, 4.76189])

In [30]: -opt['fun']   ❹
Out[30]: 3.0747286083026886
```

❶ The utility function with a negative sign to accomplish a maximization through minimization.

❷ The budget constraint as an equality constraint for the `minimize` function.

❸ The optimal consumption-saving plan, reflecting the time preference in that c_0 is higher than c_1—by exactly 10%.

❹ The maximum utility gained through the optimal plan.[1]

Expected Utility

Now consider the static two-state economy with *uncertainty*. Assume that an agent, endowed with some initial wealth, $w \in \mathbb{R}_{>0}$, gains utility only through money available in one year—but now distinguished in the two states that are possible then. This shall represent a *pure investment problem* where all available initial wealth shall be optimally invested in the traded financial assets.

Assume that *two financial assets* are traded, a risk-less bond with price process

$$B = \left(B_0, (B_1, B_1)^T\right)$$

and a risky stock with price process

$$S = \left(S_0, \left(S_1^u, S_1^d\right)^T\right)$$

Financial assets are a means to transfer the initial wealth from today to a later point in time. The major decision problem of the agent is to decide what to consume in either one of the future states.

A model for the investment problem the agent is faced with under uncertainty is given by the *expected utility* of the agent that is to be maximized given w. The *expected utility function* is given by:

$$U: \mathbb{R}_{\geq 0}^2 \to \mathbb{R}, c_1 \mapsto \mathbf{E}^P\left(u(c_1)\right)$$

---

1 Utility is only to be understood in *ordinal terms*, that is, in terms of bringing different plans into a certain order. A comparison of this numerical value with the optimal one from before does not make any sense because the utility functions are different.

With the *price vector* $\mathcal{M}_0 = (B_0, S_0)^T$, the agent can distribute their initial wealth according to

$$\mathcal{M}_0 \cdot \phi = w \iff B_0 \cdot b + S_0 \cdot s = w$$

where $\phi = (b, s)^T \in \mathbb{R}^2_{\geq 0}$ represents the *portfolio* consisting of the risk-less bond and the risky stock as composed by the agent. This *budget constraint* will always be binding due to the agent being insatiable. Short selling shall not be allowed.

The *market payoff matrix* is as follows:

$$\mathcal{M} = \begin{pmatrix} B_1 & S_1^u \\ B_1 & S_1^d \end{pmatrix}$$

How much money does the agent have available in either state one year from today? This is determined by the portfolio the agent chooses to compose:

$$c_1 = \mathcal{M} \cdot \phi = \begin{pmatrix} B_1 \\ B_1 \end{pmatrix} \cdot b + \begin{pmatrix} S_1^u \\ S_1^d \end{pmatrix} \cdot s$$

This leads to

$$c_1 = \begin{pmatrix} b \cdot B_1 + s \cdot S_1^u \\ b \cdot B_1 + s \cdot S_1^d \end{pmatrix}$$

or

$$\begin{cases} c_1^u = b \cdot B_1 + s \cdot S_1^u \\ c_1^d = b \cdot B_1 + s \cdot S_1^d \end{cases}$$

The complete decision-making problem—with regard to *optimal portfolio choice*—of the agent can then be represented as the following *constrained optimization problem*:

$$\max_{c_1} \; \mathbf{E}^P\big(u(c_1)\big)$$

(i) $w \;=\; \mathcal{M}_0 \cdot \phi$

(ii) $c_1 \;=\; \mathcal{M} \cdot \phi$

or after substituting for c_1

$$\max_{\phi} \; \mathbf{E}^P\big(u(\mathcal{M} \cdot \phi)\big)$$

$w \;=\; \mathcal{M}_0 \cdot \phi$

According to the Theorem of Lagrange, one can transform this problem into an *unconstrained optimization problem* of the form

$$\max_{b,s,\lambda} \; f(b,s,\lambda) = \mathbf{E}^P\big(u(b \cdot B_1 + s \cdot S_1)\big) - \lambda \cdot \big(b \cdot B_0 + s \cdot S_0 - w\big)$$

where the agent chooses b and s to maximize expected utility given the budget constraint.

Expected Utility Theory

Decades after its formulation and introduction, expected utility theory (EUT) is still the dominant decision-making paradigm in finance. One of its major assumptions—that agents have full knowledge of possible future states and their probabilities—is hardly ever fulfilled in reality. However, EUT is, to many, intellectually appealing and leads to "nice" results that are often easy to understand and interpret. For more on the problems with this central paradigm in finance, see Hilpisch (2020, chapters 3 and 4).

Optimal Investment Portfolio

What does an optimal solution for the expected utility maximizing agent look like? In general terms, the answer can be given based on the first-order conditions that are necessary and sufficient here for an optimal solution:

$$\begin{cases} \dfrac{\partial f}{\partial b} = 0 \\[2mm] \dfrac{\partial f}{\partial s} = 0 \\[2mm] \dfrac{\partial f}{\partial \lambda} = 0 \end{cases}$$

or

$$\frac{\partial f}{\partial b} = \quad p \cdot B_1 \cdot u'\left(b \cdot B_1 + s \cdot S_1^u\right)$$
$$+ \ (1-p) \cdot B_1 \cdot u'\left(b \cdot B_1 + s \cdot S_1^d\right) - \lambda \cdot B_0 = 0$$

and

$$\frac{\partial f}{\partial s} = \quad p \cdot S_1^u \cdot u'\left(b \cdot B_1 + s \cdot S_1^u\right)$$
$$+ \ (1-p) \cdot S_1^d \cdot u'\left(b \cdot B_1 + s \cdot S_1^d\right) - \lambda \cdot S_0 = 0$$

with the usual notation $u'(x) \equiv \frac{du}{dx}$ as well as

$$b \cdot B_0 + s \cdot S_0 = w$$

Assume logarithmic utility and for the price processes of the two traded financial assets $B = (10, 11)$ and $S = \left(10, (20, 5)^T\right)$, respectively. With $w = 10$, it holds $b + s = 1$ such that the portfolio positions represent percent values.

In Python, the `minimize` function from the `scipy.optimize` subpackage is also appropriate to solve the investment problem of the agent:

```
In [31]: B = (10, (11, 11))    ❶

In [32]: S = (10, (20, 5))    ❷

In [33]: M0 = np.array((B[0], S[0]))    ❸

In [34]: M = np.array((B[1], S[1])).T    ❹

In [35]: p = 0.5    ❺

In [36]: P = np.array((p, 1-p))    ❺

In [37]: def U(phi):
```

```
                c1 = np.dot(M, phi)  ❻
                return -np.dot(P, np.log(c1))  ❻

In [38]: -U((1, 0))  ❼
Out[38]: 2.3978952727983707

In [39]: -U((0, 1))  ❼
Out[39]: 2.3025850929940455

In [40]: -U((0.5, 0.5))  ❼
Out[40]: 2.410140782802518

In [41]: w = 10

In [42]: cons = ({'type': 'eq',
                  'fun': lambda phi: np.dot(M0, phi) - w})  ❽

In [43]: opt = minimize(U, (1, 1), constraints=cons)  ❾

In [44]: opt
Out[44]:      fun: -2.4183062699261972
              jac: array([-1.     , -0.99999])
          message: 'Optimization terminated successfully'
             nfev: 15
              nit: 5
             njev: 5
           status: 0
          success: True
                x: array([0.69442, 0.30558])

In [45]: opt['x']  ❿
Out[45]: array([0.69442, 0.30558])

In [46]: -opt['fun']  ⓫
Out[46]: 2.4183062699261972

In [47]: -U(opt['x'])  ⓫
Out[47]: 2.4183062699261972

In [48]: np.dot(M, opt['x'])  ⓬
Out[48]: array([13.75022,  9.16652])
```

❶   The bond price process and…

❷   …the stock price process.

❸   The price vector of the two traded financial assets.

❹   The market payoff matrix of the two traded financial assets.

❺   The physical probability measure for the economy.

❻ The expected utility function with logarithmic utility.

❼ Some example values for total portfolio weights of 1—diversification pays off.

❽ The budget constraint based on the dot product of the price and portfolio vectors.

❾ The expected utility maximization problem as a minimization.

❿ The optimal allocation between the bond and the stock.

⓫ The optimal expected utility value.

⓬ The state-contingent payoff from the optimal portfolio.

Time-Additive Expected Utility

It is possible to formulate the decision-making problem of the agent to include utility from money today as well:

$$U : R_{\geq 0} \times R_{\geq 0} \to \mathbb{R}, (c_0, c_1) \mapsto u(c_0) + \kappa \cdot \mathbf{E}^P(u(c_1))$$

$U : R_{\geq 0} \times R_{\geq 0} \to \mathbb{R}, (c_0, c_1) \mapsto u(c_0) + \kappa \cdot \mathbf{E}^P(u(c_1))$
With initial wealth w, the optimization problem in unconstrained form becomes:

$$\max_{c_0, b, s, \lambda} f(c_0, b, s, \lambda) = u(c_0) + \kappa \cdot \mathbf{E}^P(u(b \cdot B_1 + s \cdot S_1))$$
$$- \lambda \cdot (c_0 + b \cdot B_0 + s \cdot S_0 - w)$$

With the assumptions from before, the optimal solution is derived with Python according to the following code:

```
In [49]: M0 = np.array((1, B[0], S[0]))   ❶

In [50]: kappa = 10 / 11   ❷

In [51]: def U(phi):
             c0 = phi[0]   ❸
             c1 = np.dot(M, phi[1:])   ❸
             return -(np.log(c0) + kappa * np.dot(P, np.log(c1)))   ❸

In [52]: opt = minimize(U, (1, 1, 1), constraints=cons)

In [53]: opt
```

```
Out[53]:      fun: -3.1799295980286093
              jac: array([-0.19088, -1.90932, -1.90974])
          message: 'Optimization terminated successfully'
             nfev: 32
              nit: 8
             njev: 8
           status: 0
          success: True
                x: array([5.23899, 0.33087, 0.14523])

In [54]: -opt['fun']
Out[54]: 3.1799295980286093

In [55]: opt['x'][0]   ❹
Out[55]: 5.23898714830318

In [56]: np.dot(M, opt['x'][1:])   ❺
Out[56]: array([6.54422, 4.36571])
```

❶ The price vector including the price of 1 for consumption today.

❷ The time preference factor.

❸ The expected utility function taking into account consumption today and the time preference.

❹ This is what the agent consumes today from *w*.

❺ This is the state-contingent payoff from the bond and the stock position.

Pricing in Complete Markets

In this section, the analysis is changed to a pricing setting based on optimization principles. Assume that the two Arrow-Debreu securities are traded in the economy with two future states and that the *net supply* for both is one. The two payoff vectors form a *standard basis* for $\mathbb{R}^2$, and the market payoff matrix is:

$$\mathcal{M} = \begin{pmatrix} 1 & 0 \\ 0 & 1 \end{pmatrix}$$

Assume now that there is a *representative agent* in the economy that is the only one trading the two securities. In an *equilibrium*, the representative agent needs to hold the net supply of both securities because there is nobody else. The mechanism that ensures equilibrium is the prices of the two securities today, that is, the price vector:

$$\mathcal{M}_0 = \left(\gamma^u, \gamma^d\right)^T \in \mathbb{R}^2_{\geq 0}$$

The idea of equilibrium pricing is that this price vector needs to be adjusted in a way that the representative agent holds the net supply of all available financial assets. This is because otherwise there would be no equilibrium.

With the investment portfolio $\phi = \left(\phi^u, \phi^d\right)^T$, the problem of the expected utility maximizing, representative agent is

$$\max_{\phi} \mathbf{E}^P(u(\mathcal{M} \cdot \phi))$$
$$\text{s.t. } \mathcal{M}_0 \cdot \phi = w$$

or

$$\max_{\phi, \lambda} \mathbf{E}^P(u(\mathcal{M} \cdot \phi)) - \lambda \cdot \left(\mathcal{M}_0 \cdot \phi - w\right)$$

Due to the special market payoff matrix, this translates into

$$\max_{\phi^u, \phi^d} p \cdot u\left(\phi^u\right) + (1 - p) \cdot u\left(\phi^d\right)$$
$$\text{s.t. } \gamma^u \cdot \phi^u + \gamma^d \cdot \phi^d = w$$

and

$$\max_{\phi^u, \phi^d, \lambda} f\left(\phi^u, \phi^d, \lambda\right) = p \cdot u\left(\phi^u\right) + (1 - p) \cdot u\left(\phi^d\right) - \lambda \cdot \left(\gamma^u \cdot \phi^u + \gamma^d \cdot \phi^d - w\right)$$

The three first-order conditions for the unconstrained problem are:

$$\begin{cases} \dfrac{\partial f}{\partial \phi^u} = p \cdot u'\left(\phi^u\right) - \lambda \cdot \gamma^u = 0 \\[2mm] \dfrac{\partial f}{\partial \phi^d} = (1 - p) \cdot u'\left(\phi^d\right) - \lambda \cdot \gamma^d = 0 \\[2mm] \dfrac{\partial f}{\partial \lambda} = \gamma^u \cdot \phi^u + \gamma^d \cdot \phi^d - w = 0 \end{cases}$$

What consequences for the prices $\mathcal{M}_0$ follow from these optimality conditions? The first is with regard to the *relative price* of the two Arrow-Debreu securities:

$$\frac{\gamma^u}{\gamma^d} = \frac{p \cdot u'(\phi^u)}{(1-p) \cdot u'(\phi^d)}$$

The relative price is fully determined by the probabilities for the two states to occur and the marginal utilities gained from consumption in the two states. Factoring in that *in equilibrium* $\phi^u = \phi^d = 1$ must hold, the relative price is determined by the probability measure only:

$$\frac{\gamma^u}{\gamma^d} = \frac{p}{(1-p)}$$

With this additional condition, one also obtains:

$$\gamma^u + \gamma^d = w$$

While the relative price is determined by the probability measure in this case, the absolute prices are determined by the initial wealth available. This is intuitively appealing in that the prices should be higher the more initial wealth there is, given that the net supply for two securities is fixed.

Normalizing initial wealth to $w = 1$, for instance, fixes the prices via

$$\gamma^u = 1 - \gamma^d$$

to finally arrive at the equilibrium prices of

$$\begin{cases} \gamma^u = p \\ \gamma^d = 1 - p \end{cases}$$

or the equilibrium price vector $\mathcal{M}_0^\star = (p, 1-p)^T$.

Arbitrage Pricing

What about arbitrage prices of contingent claims given the equilibrium price vector $\mathcal{M}_0^\star$? In complete markets, in which every contingent claim is attainable, the price of any such attainable contingent claim $C_1 \in \mathbb{A} = \mathbb{R}_{\geq 0}^2$ is then given by:

$$C_0 = \mathcal{M}_0^\star \cdot C_1 = \gamma^u \cdot C_1^u + \gamma^d \cdot C_1^d$$

This is because the replication portfolio is simply the state-contingent payoff itself $\phi = C_1$ in the special case of two Arrow-Debreu securities. The prices of Arrow-Debreu securities are therefore also called *state prices* because they represent the price for one unit of currency (consumption) in a certain state.

Martingale Pricing

How does the unique martingale measure look for the current economy? The condition for the martingale measure Q is that it makes all discounted price processes of traded financial assets a martingale. In matrix form, the conditions are:

$$\mathcal{M}_0^\star = \frac{1}{1+i} \cdot \mathbf{E}^Q(\mathcal{M})$$

More explicitly, one gets:

$$\begin{cases} p \cdot (1+i) & = & q \\ (1-p) \cdot (1+i) & = & 1-q \end{cases}$$

From these, $i = 0$ follows and also $q = p$. The physical probability measure makes all probabilities already a martingale. The other way around, the prices for the two Arrow-Debreu securities are set in equilibrium in a way such that the discounted price processes are martingales.

Every attainable contingent claim $C_1 \in \mathbb{A}$ can be priced by simply taking the expectation under the physical probability measure in this special kind of representative agent economy. Formally, this translates into:

$$C_0 = \mathbf{E}^P(C_1)$$

Risk-Less Interest Rate

Why is the equilibrium risk-less interest rate zero? The answer is quite simple: because there is no risk-less financial asset traded that fixes another interest rate. Consider a *risk-less financial asset* paying 1 in every state $B_1 = (1, 1)^T$. The *arbitrage price* for this financial asset is

$$B_0 = \mathcal{M}_0^\star \cdot B_1 = p + (1-p) = 1$$

implying a risk-less interest rate of $i = 0$. Any other price $0 < B_0 < 1$, implying a positive risk-less interest rate, would also imply arbitrage opportunities.

A Numerical Example (I)

The equilibrium pricing analysis so far rests on a number of simplifying assumptions allowing for elegant solutions and simple relations. Consider now a case with the somehow more realistic numerical assumptions as used multiple times before.

Specifically, assume expected utility maximization based on logarithmic utility for the representative agent. Assume further price processes for the risk-less bond of

$$B = \left(B_0, (11, 11)^T\right)$$

and for the risky stock of

$$S = \left(S_0, (20, 5)^T\right)$$

The market payoff matrix accordingly is:

$$\mathcal{M} = \begin{pmatrix} 11 & 20 \\ 11 & 5 \end{pmatrix}$$

The physical probability measure is given by $P = (p, (1 - p))^T$ with $p = \frac{1}{3}$. The net supply of the risk-less bond is $b = 1$, and it is $s = 1$ for the risky stock. The initial wealth the agent has available shall be $w = 15$.

The problem of the representative agent is

$$\max_{\phi, \lambda} f(\phi, \lambda) = \mathbf{E}^P(u(\mathcal{M} \cdot \phi)) - \lambda \cdot (\mathcal{M}_0 \cdot \phi - w)$$

or

$$\max_{b, s, \lambda} f(b, s, \lambda) = \mathbf{E}^P\left(u(b \cdot B_1 + s \cdot S_1)\right) - \lambda \cdot (b \cdot B_0 + s \cdot S_0 - w)$$

The three first-order conditions are:

$$\begin{cases} \frac{\partial f}{\partial b} = \mathbf{E}^P\left(B_1 \cdot u'(b \cdot B_1 + s \cdot S_1)\right) - \lambda \cdot B_0 = 0 \\ \frac{\partial f}{\partial s} = \mathbf{E}^P\left(S_1 \cdot u'(b \cdot B_1 + s \cdot S_1)\right) - \lambda \cdot S_0 = 0 \\ \frac{\partial f}{\partial \lambda} = b \cdot B_0 + s \cdot S_0 - w = 0 \end{cases}$$

The *relative price* for the two financial assets according to the optimality conditions—and taking into account the net supply of one for both financial assets as well as the logarithmic utility—is:

$$\frac{S_0}{B_0} = \frac{\mathbf{E}^P\big(S_1 \cdot u'(b \cdot B_1 + s \cdot S_1)\big)}{\mathbf{E}^P\big(B_1 \cdot u'(b \cdot B_1 + s \cdot S_1)\big)}$$

$$= \frac{\mathbf{E}^P\left(\dfrac{S_1}{B_1 + S_1}\right)}{\mathbf{E}^P\left(\dfrac{B_1}{B_1 + S_1}\right)} \equiv \zeta$$

Adding the budget constraint to the mix fixes not only the *relative price* ζ but also the absolute price levels:

$$B_0 + \zeta \cdot B_0 = w \Longleftrightarrow B_0 = \frac{w}{1 + \zeta}$$

In Python, these considerations translate into simple vectorized operations using NumPy:

```
In [57]: p = 1 / 3    ❶

In [58]: P = np.array((p, (1-p)))    ❶

In [59]: B1 = np.array((11, 11))

In [60]: S1 = np.array((20, 5))

In [61]: zeta = np.dot(S1 / (B1 + S1), P) / np.dot(B1 / (B1 + S1), P)    ❷

In [62]: zeta    ❷
Out[62]: 0.7342657342657343

In [63]: w = 15    ❸

In [64]: B0 = w / (1 + zeta)    ❹

In [65]: B0    ❹
Out[65]: 8.649193548387098

In [66]: S0 = zeta * B0    ❺

In [67]: S0    ❺
Out[67]: 6.350806451612904

In [68]: B0 + S0    ❻
```

```
Out[68]: 15.000000000000002

In [69]: i = B1.mean() / B0 - 1  ❼

In [70]: i  ❼
Out[70]: 0.2717948717948717

In [71]: mu = np.dot(S1, P) / S0 - 1  ❽

In [72]: mu  ❽
Out[72]: 0.5746031746031743
```

❶ The probability measure.

❷ The price ratio zeta given optimality conditions.

❸ The initial wealth.

❹ The equilibrium price level of the risk-less bond given the price ratio zeta and initial wealth w.

❺ The resulting equilibrium price level of the risky stock.

❻ The budget constraint is binding.

❼ The equilibrium interest rate given the price level for the risk-less bond.

❽ The equilibrium expected rate of return of the risky stock.

Equilibrium pricing does not lead in this case to the discounted price processes being martingales under the physical probability measure. The *martingale measure* is easily derived, however. The analysis uses the SymPy (*http://sympy.org*) package for symbolic computations with Python:

```
In [73]: import sympy as sy  ❶

In [74]: q = sy.Symbol('q')  ❷

In [75]: eq = (q * 20 + (1 - q) * 5) / (1 + i) - S0  ❸

In [76]: eq  ❹
Out[76]: 11.7943548387097*q - 2.41935483870968

In [77]: q = sy.solve(eq)[0]  ❺

In [78]: q  ❻
Out[78]: 0.205128205128205

In [79]: Q = np.array((q, 1 - q))  ❻
```

```
In [80]: np.dot(B1, Q) / (1 + i)   ➐
Out[80]: 8.64919354838710

In [81]: np.dot(S1, Q) / (1 + i)   ➐
Out[81]: 6.35080645161290
```

➊ Imports the symbolic computation package SymPy.

➋ Defining the symbol q.

➌ Formulating the equation for q given the martingale condition.

➍ The equation simplified.

➎ This solves the equation numerically.

➏ The resulting martingale measure.

➐ Both discounted price processes are martingales under Q.

Pricing in Incomplete Markets

How does representative agent pricing work in *incomplete markets*? The answer fortunately is: exactly the same way as in complete markets.

Assume the two date, three-state economy in which a *risk-less bond* with price process

$$B = \left(B_0, (11, 11, 11)^T\right)$$

and a *risky stock* with price process

$$S = \left(S_0, (20, 10, 5)^T\right)$$

are traded. The physical probability measure is $P = (p, p, p)^T$, with $p = \frac{1}{3}$. Everything else shall be as in the previous section.

Formally, the optimization problem of the representative agent does not change:

$$\max_{b, s, \lambda} f(b, s, \lambda) = \mathbf{E}^P\left(u\left(b \cdot B_1 + s \cdot S_1\right)\right) - \lambda \cdot \left(b \cdot B_0 + s \cdot S_0 - w\right)$$

Nor does the formula for the relative price change:

$$\frac{S_0}{B_0} = \frac{\mathbf{E}^P\left(\frac{S_1}{B_1 + S_1}\right)}{\mathbf{E}^P\left(\frac{B_1}{B_1 + S_1}\right)} \equiv \zeta$$

In Python, only the future price vectors of the financial assets and the vector representing the probability measure need to be adjusted:

```
In [82]: p = 1 / 3  ❶

In [83]: P = np.array((p, p, p))  ❶

In [84]: B1 = np.array((11, 11, 11))

In [85]: S1 = np.array((20, 10, 5))

In [86]: zeta = np.dot(S1 / (B1 + S1), P) / np.dot(B1 / (B1 + S1), P)  ❷

In [87]: zeta  ❷
Out[87]: 0.9155274934101636

In [88]: w = 15  ❸

In [89]: B0 = w / (1 + zeta)  ❹

In [90]: B0  ❹
Out[90]: 7.8307411674347165

In [91]: S0 = zeta * B0  ❺

In [92]: S0  ❺
Out[92]: 7.169258832565284

In [93]: B0 + S0  ❻
Out[93]: 15.0

In [94]: i = B1.mean() / B0 - 1  ❼

In [95]: i  ❼
Out[95]: 0.40472016183411985

In [96]: mu = np.dot(S1, P) / S0 - 1  ❽

In [97]: mu  ❽
Out[97]: 0.6273183796451287
```

❶ The probability measure.

❷ The relative price zeta given optimality conditions.

❸ The initial wealth.

❹ The equilibrium price level of the risk-less bond given the price ratio `zeta` and initial wealth `w`.

❺ The resulting equilibrium price level of the risky stock.

❻ The budget constraint is binding.

❼ The equilibrium interest rate given the price level for the risk-less bond.

❽ The equilibrium expected rate of return of the risky stock.

Representative Agent Pricing

The pricing of securities based on the optimization calculus of a representative agent is one approach that applies to both complete and incomplete markets. Instead of adjusting markets—for example, via market completion based on additional securities—additional assumptions are made with regard to the representative agent. For example, the initial wealth of the agent is required to arrive at specific, absolute prices for the securities instead of only relative prices.

Martingale Measures

Although representative agent pricing works in incomplete markets the same way as in complete ones, it unfortunately does not directly solve the problem of pricing contingent claims that are not attainable. There are still infinitely many martingale measures that are consistent with the market.

The Python code that follows shows that there are infinitely many martingale measures that are consistent with the equilibrium price processes as derived in the previous section:

```
In [98]: qu = sy.Symbol('qu')    ❶
         qm = sy.Symbol('qm')    ❶

In [99]: eq = (qu * 20 + qm * 10 + (1 - qu - qm) * 5) / (1 + i) - S0    ❷

In [100]: eq    ❸
Out[100]: 3.55942780337942*qm + 10.6782834101383*qu - 3.60983102918587

In [101]: Q = sy.solve(eq, set=True)    ❹

In [102]: Q    ❺
Out[102]: ([qm], {(1.01416048550236 - 3.00000000000001*qu,)})
```

❶ Defining the symbols qu and qm.

❷ Formulating the equation for qu and qm given the martingale condition.

❸ The equation simplified.

❹ This solves the equation numerically, providing a set of solutions as the result; this does not take into account the conditions $0 \leq q^u, q^d \leq 1$.

❺ The relationship between qu and qm as the solution—indicating infinitely many solutions.

Martingale Measure in Incomplete Markets

Martingale pricing is a convenient and elegant approach in complete markets to value contingent claims. In incomplete markets, there are in general *infinitely many* martingale measures that are consistent with the market. In practice, one often solves this issue by relying on publicly observed market prices for liquidly trading contingent claims, such as plain vanilla European put or call options. These prices are used to calibrate model parameters or the martingale measure directly to be consistent with the market. For more background information and details about model calibration, see Hilpisch (2015).

Equilibrium Pricing

What about pricing contingent claims? If they are *attainable* through replication portfolios composed of traded financial assets, their price can be fixed by the *usual arbitrage argument*. What if a contingent claim is *not attainable*? In the simple incomplete market setting currently under investigation, this can only mean that the payoff vector is linearly independent of the two future price vectors of the traded financial assets. This in turn implies that the introduction of a contingent claim with such a payoff vector is *market completing*—because three linearly independent vectors form in any case a basis of $\mathbb{R}^3$.

Consider the market payoff matrix from the first two Arrow-Debreu securities, each available at a net supply of one:

$$\mathcal{M} = \begin{pmatrix} 1 & 0 \\ 0 & 1 \\ 0 & 0 \end{pmatrix}$$

This market is obviously incomplete because the two securities do not span $\mathbb{R}^3$. Introducing a contingent claim with net supply of one that pays one unit of currency in the d state—that is, a contingent claim that pays exactly what the third Arrow-Debreu security would pay—completes the market as seen by the resulting payoff matrix:

$$\mathcal{M} = \begin{pmatrix} 1 & 0 & 0 \\ 0 & 1 & 0 \\ 0 & 0 & 1 \end{pmatrix}$$

The three payoff vectors now form a standard basis of the $\mathbb{R}^3$.

Formally, the optimization problem of the representative agent is the same as before:

$$\max_{\phi} \mathbf{E}^P(u(\mathcal{M} \cdot \phi))$$

$$\text{s.t. } \mathcal{M}_0 \cdot \phi = w$$

Here, $\mathcal{M}_0 = \left(\gamma^u, \gamma^m, \gamma^d\right)^T$ as the state price vector and $\phi = (1, 1, 1)^T$ as the market portfolio.

In explicit form, the unconstrained optimization problem according to the Theorem of Lagrange is:

$$\max_{\phi^u, \phi^m, \phi^d, \lambda} f\left(\phi^u, \phi^m, \phi^d, \lambda\right) = p^u \cdot u\left(\phi^u\right) + p^m \cdot u\left(\phi^m\right) + p^d \cdot u\left(\phi^d\right)$$

$$- \lambda \cdot \left(\gamma^u \cdot \phi^u + \gamma^m \cdot \phi^m + \gamma^d \cdot \phi^d - w\right)$$

The four first-order conditions for the unconstrained problem are:

$$\begin{cases} \dfrac{\partial f}{\partial \phi^u} = p^u \cdot u'\left(\phi^u\right) - \lambda \cdot \gamma^u = 0 \\[2mm] \dfrac{\partial f}{\partial \phi^m} = p^m \cdot u'\left(\phi^m\right) - \lambda \cdot \gamma^m = 0 \\[2mm] \dfrac{\partial f}{\partial \phi^d} = p^d \cdot u'\left(\phi^d\right) - \lambda \cdot \gamma^d = 0 \\[2mm] \dfrac{\partial f}{\partial \lambda} = \gamma^u \cdot \phi^u + \gamma^m \cdot \phi^m + \gamma^d \cdot \phi^d - w = 0 \end{cases}$$

For the relative prices, one gets:

$$\begin{cases} \dfrac{\gamma^u}{\gamma^m} = \dfrac{p^u \cdot u'(\phi^u)}{p^m \cdot u'(\phi^m)} \\[2ex] \dfrac{\gamma^u}{\gamma^d} = \dfrac{p^u \cdot u'(\phi^u)}{p^d \cdot u'(\phi^d)} \end{cases}$$

Through these, the third relative price is fixed as well. With logarithmic utility and an initial wealth fixed at $w = 1$, one finally arrives in this special case at:

$$\begin{cases} \gamma^u = p^u \\ \gamma^m = p^m \\ \gamma^d = p^d \end{cases}$$

The equilibrium price vector is $\mathcal{M}_0^\star = \left(p^u, p^m, p^d\right)^T$, which equals the vector representing the probability measure. This in turn implies that all discounted price processes are martingales under the physical probability measure.

A Numerical Example (II)

Getting back to the numerical example from before: assume expected utility maximization based on *logarithmic utility* for the representative agent. Assume further price processes for the *risk-less bond* of

$$B = \left(B_0, (11, 11, 11)^T\right)$$

and for the *risky stock* of

$$S = \left(S_0, (20, 10, 5)^T\right)$$

The market payoff matrix is:

$$\mathcal{M} = \begin{pmatrix} 11 & 20 \\ 11 & 10 \\ 11 & 5 \end{pmatrix}$$

The physical probability measure is given by $P = (p, p, p)^T$, with $p = \frac{1}{3}$. The net supply of the risk-less bond is $b = 1$, and it is $s = 1$ for the risky stock. The initial wealth the agent has available shall be $w = 15$.

A contingent claim is introduced with payoff $C_1 = (5, 0, 0)^T$ and a net supply of $c = 1$.

Consequently, the problem of the representative agent is:

$$\max_{\phi, \lambda} f(\phi, \lambda) = \mathbf{E}^P(u(\mathcal{M} \cdot \phi)) - \lambda \cdot (\mathcal{M}_0 \cdot \phi - w)$$

or

$$\max_{b, s, c, \lambda} f(b, s, \lambda) = \mathbf{E}^P(u(b \cdot B_1 + s \cdot S_1 + c \cdot C_1)) - \lambda \cdot (b \cdot B_0 + s \cdot S_0 + c \cdot C_0 - w)$$

The four first-order conditions are:

$$\begin{cases} \dfrac{\partial f}{\partial b} = \mathbf{E}^P(B_1 \cdot u'(b \cdot B_1 + s \cdot S_1 + c \cdot C_1)) - \lambda \cdot B_0 = 0 \\[2mm] \dfrac{\partial f}{\partial s} = \mathbf{E}^P(S_1 \cdot u'(b \cdot B_1 + s \cdot S_1 + c \cdot C_1)) - \lambda \cdot S_0 = 0 \\[2mm] \dfrac{\partial f}{\partial c} = \mathbf{E}^P(C_1 \cdot u'(b \cdot B_1 + s \cdot S_1 + c \cdot C_1)) - \lambda \cdot C_0 = 0 \\[2mm] \dfrac{\partial f}{\partial \lambda} = b \cdot B_0 + s \cdot S_0 + c \cdot C_0 - w = 0 \end{cases}$$

The *relative prices* for the three financial assets are fixed through:

$$\begin{cases} \dfrac{S_0}{B_0} = \dfrac{\mathbf{E}^P\left(\dfrac{S_1}{B_1 + S_1 + C_1}\right)}{\mathbf{E}^P\left(\dfrac{B_1}{B_1 + S_1 + C_1}\right)} \equiv \zeta_1 \\[6mm] \dfrac{C_0}{B_0} = \dfrac{\mathbf{E}^P\left(\dfrac{C_1}{B_1 + S_1 + C_1}\right)}{\mathbf{E}^P\left(\dfrac{B_1}{B_1 + S_1 + C_1}\right)} \equiv \zeta_2 \end{cases}$$

Adding the *budget constraint* to the mix fixes not only the relative prices ζ_1 and ζ_2 but also the absolute price levels:

$$B_0 + \zeta_1 \cdot B_0 + \zeta_2 \cdot B_0 = w \Longleftrightarrow B_0 = \frac{w}{1 + \zeta_1 + \zeta_2}$$

The adjustments to the Python code are only minor compared to the complete markets case:

```
In [103]: p = 1 / 3   ❶

In [104]: P = np.array((p, p, p))   ❶

In [105]: B1 = np.array((11, 11, 11))   ❷

In [106]: S1 = np.array((20, 10, 5))   ❷

In [107]: C1 = np.array((5, 0, 0))   ❷

In [108]: zeta_1 = (np.dot(S1 / (B1 + S1 + C1), P) /
                    np.dot(B1 / (B1 + S1 + C1), P))   ❸

In [109]: zeta_1   ❸
Out[109]: 0.8862001308044474

In [110]: zeta_2 = (np.dot(C1 / (B1 + S1 + C1), P) /
                    np.dot(B1 / (B1 + S1 + C1), P))   ❹

In [111]: zeta_2   ❹
Out[111]: 0.09156311314584695

In [112]: w = 15   ❺

In [113]: B0 = w / (1 + zeta_1 + zeta_2)   ❻

In [114]: B0   ❻
Out[114]: 7.584325396825396

In [115]: S0 = zeta_1 * B0   ❼

In [116]: S0   ❼
Out[116]: 6.721230158730158

In [117]: C0 = zeta_2 * B0   ❽

In [118]: C0   ❽
Out[118]: 0.6944444444444443

In [119]: B0 + S0 + C0   ❾
Out[119]: 14.999999999999998

In [120]: i = B1.mean() / B0 - 1   ❿

In [121]: i   ❿
```

```
Out[121]: 0.45035971223021587

In [122]: muS = np.dot(S1, P) / S0 - 1  ⓫

In [123]: muS  ⓫
Out[123]: 0.7357933579335794

In [124]: muC = np.dot(C1, P) / C0 - 1  ⓬

In [125]: muC  ⓬
Out[125]: 1.4000000000000004
```

❶ The probability measure.

❷ The payoff vectors.

❸ The first relative price.

❹ The second relative price.

❺ The initial wealth…

❻ …and the resulting price for the risk-less bond.

❼ The equilibrium price for the risky stock.

❽ The equilibrium price for the contingent claim.

❾ The budget constraint is binding.

❿ The risk-less interest rate.

⓫ The equilibrium expected rate of return for the risky stock.

⓬ The equilibrium expected rate of return for the contingent claim.

That the introduction of the contingent claim—as a third traded financial asset—is market completing can be seen by the fact that there is now a unique martingale measure:

```
In [126]: M = np.array((B1, S1, C1)).T  ❶

In [127]: M  ❶
Out[127]: array([[11, 20,  5],
                 [11, 10,  0],
                 [11,  5,  0]])

In [128]: M0 = np.array((B0, S0, C0))  ❷
```

```
In [129]: Q = np.linalg.solve(M.T / (1 + i), M0)   ❸

In [130]: Q   ❹
Out[130]: array([0.20144, 0.34532, 0.45324])

In [131]: sum(Q)   ❹
Out[131]: 1.0

In [132]: np.allclose(np.dot(M.T, Q), M0 * (1 + i))   ❺
Out[132]: True
```

❶   The new market payoff matrix including the contingent claim.

❷   The vector with the prices of the three financial assets/contingent claims.

❸   This solves for the vector Q representing the martingale measure Q (note the use of the transpose operator .T).

❹   The solution vector whose components add up to 1.

❺   A final check whether all discounted price processes are indeed martingales.

Conclusions

This chapter is concerned with the modeling of agents and their optimization problems, mainly on the basis of the expected utility maximization approach. Two central topics are discussed: *optimal portfolio choice* and *equilibrium pricing of financial assets and contingent claims* in complete and incomplete markets. While in the first case the prices are given and the quantities in the investment portfolio are chosen, in the latter case the quantities to be held in the investment portfolio are fixed, and the prices are adjusted for this to be optimal for the representative agent. Python proves once again a powerful ecosystem with helpful packages to model and solve the related optimization problems.

Although the model economies in this and the previous two chapters are admittedly simplistic, the techniques and methods introduced carry over to *general static model economies*, that is, those having many more—even countably infinite—different future states (instead of two or three only). With some additional formalism, they even carry over to *dynamic economies* with many—potentially countably infinite—relevant points in time (instead of just two).

Further Resources

Books cited in this chapter:

Duffie, Darrell. 1988. *Security Markets—Stochastic Models*. San Diego: Academic Press.

Eichberger, Jürgen and Ian Harper. 1997. *Financial Economics*. New York: Oxford University Press.

Hilpisch, Yves. 2020. *Artificial Intelligence in Finance*. Sebastopol: O'Reilly.

Hilpisch, Yves. 2015. *Derivatives Analytics with Python*. Wiley Finance.

Markowitz, Harry. 1959. *Portfolio Selection—Efficient Diversification of Investments*. New York: John Wiley & Sons.

Milne, Frank. 1995. *Finance Theory and Asset Pricing*. New York: Oxford University Press.

Sundaram, Rangarajan. 1996. *A First Course in Optimization Theory*. Cambridge University Press, Cambridge.

Varian, Hal. 1992. *Microeconomic Analysis*. 3rd ed. New York and London: W.W. Norton & Company.

## CHAPTER 5

Static Economy

A securities market model is viable if and only if there exists at least one equivalent martingale measure for it.

—Harrison and Kreps (1979)

The central piece of the theory relating the no-arbitrage arguments with martingale theory is the so-called Fundamental Theorem of Asset Pricing.

—Delbaen and Schachermayer (2006)

This chapter introduces more formalism to model a general static economy. Such an economy is characterized by an arbitrarily large, but still finite, state space. As before, the general static economy is analyzed at two relevant points in time only, for example, today and one year from now. Therefore, this chapter introduces one major generalization—namely with regard to the state space. The next chapter then generalizes the model economy further with regard to the number of relevant points in time. This enables one to also model dynamics.

The chapter makes use, as before, of linear algebra and probability theoretical concepts. Books that cover these topics well for the purposes of this chapter are Aleskerov et al. (2011) for linear algebra and Jacod and Protter (2004) for probability theory. A gentle introduction to general static economies and their analysis is found in Milne (1995). Pliska (1997) is a good introductory textbook on the topic that is both accessible and rigorous. Duffie (1988) is an advanced text that covers general static economies in greater detail, providing all the necessary tools from linear algebra and probability in a self-contained fashion.

Topics covered in this chapter are general discrete probability spaces, financial assets and contingent claims, market completeness, the two Fundamental Theorems of Asset Pricing, replication and arbitrage pricing, Black-Scholes-Merton (1973) and Merton (1976) option pricing, and representative agent pricing with Arrow-Debreu securities. The following table gives an overview of the topics in finance, mathematics, and Python found in this chapter:

Finance	Mathematics	Python
Uncertainty	State space, algebra, probability measure, probability space	NumPy, ndarray, rng.normal
Financial asset, contingent claim	Random variable, expectation	rng, mean(), np.dot
Market payoff matrix	Matrix	ndarray, mean(), std()
Replication, arbitrage pricing	Solving systems of linear equations, dot product	np.maximum, np.linalg.solve, np.dot
Market completeness	Rank, span, vector space	ndarray, np.dot, np.linalg.matrix_rank
Martingale measure	Probability measure	ndarray, scipy.optimize.minimize
Black-Scholes-Merton model (1973)	Geometric Brownian motion, normal distribution, Monte Carlo simulation, replication	rng.standard_normal, np.linalg.lstsq
Merton (1976) model, log-normal jumps	Jump diffusion, Poisson distribution	rng.poisson, np.linalg.lstsq

The major goal of this chapter is *generalization*. Almost all of the concepts and notions presented in this chapter have been introduced in the previous chapters. The enlargement of the state space makes the introduction of a bit more formalism necessary. However, on the Python side, the code is still as concise as experienced before. The benefits of this generalization should be clear. It is simply not realistic to model the possible future share price of, say, the Apple stock with two or three states only. It is much more realistic to assume that the share price can take on a value out of a possible 100, 500, or even more values. This is an important step toward a more realistic financial model.

Uncertainty

Consider an economy with a *general, discrete state space* Ω with a finite number of elements $|\Omega| < \infty$. An *algebra* $\mathcal{F}$ in Ω is a family of sets for which the following statements hold true:

1. $\Omega \in \mathcal{F}$

2. $\mathbb{E} \in \mathcal{F} \Rightarrow \mathbb{E}^c \in \mathcal{F}$

3. $\mathbb{E}_1, \mathbb{E}_2, \ldots, \mathbb{E}_I \in \mathcal{F} \Rightarrow \cup_{i=1}^{I} \mathbb{E}_i \in \mathcal{F}$

$\mathbb{E}^c$ denotes the complement of a set $\mathbb{E}$. The power set $\wp(\Omega)$ is the largest algebra, while the set $\mathcal{F} = \{\emptyset, \Omega\}$ is the smallest algebra in Ω. An algebra is a model for *observable events* in an economy. In this context, a single state of the economy $\omega \in \Omega$ can be interpreted as an *atomic event*.

A *probability* assigns a real number $0 \leq p_\omega \equiv P(\{\omega\}) \leq 1$ to a state $\omega \in \Omega$ or a real number $0 \leq P(\mathbb{E}) \leq 1$ to an event $\mathbb{E} \in \mathcal{F}$. If the probabilities for all states are known, one has $P(\mathbb{E}) = \Sigma_{\omega \in \mathbb{E}} p_\omega$.

A *probability measure* $P: \mathcal{F} \to [0, 1]$ is characterized by the following characteristics:

1. $\forall \mathbb{E} \in \mathcal{F}: P(\mathbb{E}) \geq 0$
2. $P\left(\cup_{i=1}^{I} \mathbb{E}_i\right) = \Sigma_{i=1}^{I} \mathbb{E}_i$ for disjoint sets $\mathbb{E}_i \in \mathcal{F}$
3. $P(\Omega) = 1$

Together the three elements $\{\Omega, \mathcal{F}, P\}$ form a *probability space*. A probability space is the formal representation of *uncertainty* in the model economy.

Random Variables

Given a probability space $\{\Omega, \mathcal{F}, P\}$, a *random variable* is a $\mathcal{F}$ −measurable function:

$$S: \Omega \to \mathbb{R}_{\geq 0}, \omega \mapsto S(\omega)$$

$\mathcal{F}$ −measurability implies that for each $\mathbb{E} \in \{[a, b[: a, b \in \mathbb{R}, a < b\}$, one has:

$$S^{-1}(\mathbb{E}) \equiv \{\omega \in \Omega: S(\omega) \in \mathbb{E}\} \in \mathcal{F}$$

If $\mathcal{F} \equiv \mathcal{P}(\Omega)$, the *expectation* of a random variable is defined by:

$$\mathbf{E}^P(S) = \sum_{\omega \in \Omega} P(\omega) \cdot S(\omega)$$

Otherwise, it holds:

$$\mathbf{E}^P(S) = \sum_{\mathbb{E} \in \mathcal{F}} P(\mathbb{E}) \cdot S(\mathbb{E})$$

Numerical Examples

To make a concrete example, assume a state space of $\Omega = \{\omega_1, \omega_2, \omega_3, \omega_4\}$. Furthermore, assume that an algebra with $\mathscr{F} = \{\emptyset, \{\omega_1, \omega_2\}, \{\omega_3, \omega_4\}, \Omega\}$ is given. It is easily verified that this set satisfies the three characteristics of an algebra in Ω. The probability measure shall be defined by $P(\{\omega_1, \omega_2\}) = P(\{\omega_3, \omega_4\}) = \frac{1}{2}$. Again, it is easy to see that P is indeed a probability measure on $\mathscr{F}$ under these assumptions.

Consider now a function T with $T(\omega_1) = 1, T(\omega_2) = 2, T(\omega_3) = 3$, and $T(\omega_4) = 4$. This function is *not* a random variable defined on the probability space since the algebra $\mathscr{F}$ does not distinguish, for example, between ω_1 and ω_2—they are subsumed by the set $\{\omega_1, \omega_2\}$. One could say that the algebra is "not granular" enough.

Consider another function S with $S(\omega_1) = 20, S(\omega_2) = 20, S(\omega_3) = 5$, and $S(\omega_4) = 5$. This is now a random variable defined on the probability space with an expectation of:

$$\mathbf{E}^P(S) = \sum_{\mathbb{E} \in \mathscr{F}} P(\mathbb{E}) \cdot S(\mathbb{E}) = \frac{1}{2} \cdot 20 + \frac{1}{2} \cdot 5 = 12.5$$

In general, however, it will be assumed that $\mathscr{F} \equiv \wp(\Omega)$, with P accordingly defined such that the function (random variable) T, for example, also is $\mathscr{F}$–measurable with the expectation properly defined.

With Python, it is efficient to illustrate cases in which Ω is much larger. The following Python code assumes equal probability for all possible states:

```
In [1]: import numpy as np
        from numpy.random import default_rng
        np.set_printoptions(precision=5, suppress=True)

In [2]: rng = default_rng(100)   ❶

In [3]: I = 1000   ❷

In [4]: S = rng.normal(loc=100, scale=20, size=I)   ❸

In [5]: S[:14]   ❸
Out[5]: array([ 76.84901, 105.79512, 115.61708, 110.87947,  80.77235, 121.42017,
               114.02911, 114.09947, 114.90125, 122.08694, 144.85945,  87.77014,
               100.94422, 135.08469])

In [6]: S.mean()   ❹
Out[6]: 100.88376804485935
```

❶ Fixes the seed value for the NumPy random number generator for reproducibility of the results.

❷ Fixes the number of states in the state space (for the simulations to follow).

❸ Draws I normally distributed (pseudo-)random numbers with mean `loc` and standard deviation `scale`.

❹ Calculates the expectation (mean value) assuming an equal probability for every simulated value (state).

Any other probability measure can, of course, also be chosen:

```
In [7]: P = rng.random(I)   ❶

In [8]: P[:10]   ❷
Out[8]: array([0.34914, 0.33408, 0.41319, 0.06102, 0.6339 , 0.51285, 0.51177,
               0.92149, 0.72853, 0.58985])

In [9]: P /= P.sum()   ❷

In [10]: P.sum()   ❷
Out[10]: 1.0

In [11]: P[:10]   ❸
Out[11]: array([0.00072, 0.00069, 0.00085, 0.00013, 0.00131, 0.00106, 0.00106,
               0.0019 , 0.0015 , 0.00122])

In [12]: np.dot(P, S)   ❹
Out[12]: 100.71981640185018
```

❶ Draws uniformly distributed random numbers between 0 and 1.

❷ Normalizes the values in the `ndarray` object to sum up to 1.

❸ The resulting weights according to the random probability measure.

❹ The expectation as the dot product of the probability vector and the vector representing the random variable.

Mathematical Techniques

In addition to linear algebra, traditional probability theory plays a central role in discrete finance. It allows us to capture and analyze uncertainty and, more specifically, risk in a systematic, well-established way. When moving from discrete finance models to continuous ones, more advanced approaches, such as stochastic calculus, are required. For discrete finance models, standard linear algebra and probability theory prove powerful enough in most cases. For more details on discrete finance, refer to Pliska (1997).

Financial Assets

Consider an economy at two different dates $t \in \{0, 1\}$, today and one year from now (or any other time period in the future to this end). Assume that a probability space $\{\Omega, \mathscr{F} \equiv \wp(\Omega), P\}$ is given that represents *uncertainty* about the future in the model economy, with $|\Omega| \equiv I$ possible future states. In this case, $\Omega = \{\omega_1, \omega_2, \ldots, \omega_I\}$.

A traded *financial asset* is represented by a price process $S = (S_0, S_1)$, where the price today is fixed $S_0 \in \mathbb{R}_{>0}$, and the price in one year, $S_1 : \Omega \to \mathbb{R}_{\geq 0}$, is a random variable that is $\mathscr{F}$–measurable. Formally, the future price vector of a traded financial asset is a vector with I elements:

$$S_1 = \begin{pmatrix} S_1(\omega_1) \\ S_1(\omega_2) \\ \cdots \\ S_1(\omega_I) \end{pmatrix}$$

If there are multiple financial assets traded, say $K > 1$, they are represented by multiple price processes, $S^k = (S_0^k, S_1^k), k = 1, 2, \ldots, K$. The *market payoff matrix* is then composed of the future price vectors of the traded financial assets:

$$\mathscr{M} = \begin{pmatrix} S_1^1(\omega_1) & S_1^2(\omega_1) & \cdots & S_1^K(\omega_1) \\ S_1^1(\omega_2) & S_1^2(\omega_2) & \cdots & S_1^K(\omega_2) \\ \cdots & \cdots & \cdots & \cdots \\ S_1^1(\omega_3) & S_1^2(\omega_3) & \cdots & S_1^K(\omega_3) \end{pmatrix}$$

Denote the *set of traded financial assets* by $\mathscr{S} \equiv (S^1, S^2, \ldots, S^K)$. The *static model economy* can then be summarized by

$$\mathcal{E} = (\{\Omega, \mathcal{F}, P\}, \mathcal{S})$$

where it is usually assumed that $\mathcal{F} \equiv \wp(\Omega)$.

Fixing the number of possible future states to five $\Omega = \{\omega_1, \ldots, \omega_5\}$ with equal probability $\forall \omega \in \Omega : P(\omega) = \frac{1}{5}$ and the number of traded financial assets to five as well, a numerical example in Python illustrates such a static model economy:

```
In [13]: M = np.array((
              (11, 25, 0,  0,  25),
              (11, 20, 30, 15, 25),
              (11, 10, 0,  20, 10),
              (11, 5,  30, 15, 0),
              (11, 0,  0,  0,  0)
         ))  ❶

In [14]: M0 = np.array(5 * [10.])  ❷

In [15]: M0  ❷
Out[15]: array([10., 10., 10., 10., 10.])

In [16]: M.mean(axis=0)  ❸
Out[16]: array([11., 12., 12., 10., 12.])

In [17]: mu = M.mean(axis=0) / M0 - 1  ❹

In [18]: mu  ❹
Out[18]: array([0.1, 0.2, 0.2, 0. , 0.2])

In [19]: (M / M0 - 1)  ❺
Out[19]: array([[ 0.1,  1.5, -1. , -1. ,  1.5],
               [ 0.1,  1. ,  2. ,  0.5,  1.5],
               [ 0.1,  0. , -1. ,  1. ,  0. ],
               [ 0.1, -0.5,  2. ,  0.5, -1. ],
               [ 0.1, -1. , -1. , -1. , -1. ]])

In [20]: sigma = (M / M0 - 1).std(axis=0)  ❻

In [21]: sigma  ❻
Out[21]: array([0.     , 0.92736, 1.46969, 0.83666, 1.1225 ])
```

❶ The assumed market payoff matrix where the columns represent the future, uncertain price vectors of the traded financial assets.

❷ The current price vector for the five assets, for each of which the price is fixed to 10.

❸ This calculates the expected (or average) future price for every traded financial asset.

❹ This in turn calculates the expected (or average) rates of return.

❺ The rates of return matrix calculated and printed out.

❻ The standard deviation of the rates of return or volatility calculated for every traded financial asset—the first one is risk-less; it can be considered to be a bond.

Contingent Claims

Given a model economy $\mathcal{E}$, a *contingent claim* is characterized by a price process
$C = (C_0, C_1)$, where C_1 is an $\mathcal{F}$ –measurable random variable.

One can think of European call and put options as canonical examples of contingent
claims. The payoff of a European call option might, for instance, be defined relative to
the second traded financial asset according to $C_1 = \max\left(S_1^2 - K, 0\right)$, where $K \in \mathbb{R}_{\geq 0}$
is the strike price of the option. Since the payoff of the option is "derived" from
another asset, one therefore often speaks of *derivative instruments*, or *derivatives* for
short.

If a contingent claim can be *replicated* by a portfolio $\phi \in \mathbb{R}^K$ of the traded financial
assets $\mathcal{S}$

$$\mathcal{M} \cdot \phi = C_1$$

then the *arbitrage price* of the contingent claim is

$$\mathcal{M}_0 \cdot \phi = C_0$$

where $\mathcal{M}_0 = \left(S_0^1, S_0^2, \ldots, S_0^K\right)^T \in \mathbb{R}_{>0}^I$ is the *current price vector* of the traded financial
assets.

Continuing the Python example from before, replication of contingent claims based
on linear algebra methods is illustrated in the following:

```
In [22]: K = 15   ❶

In [23]: M[:, 1]   ❶
Out[23]: array([25, 20, 10,  5,  0])

In [24]: C1 = np.maximum(M[:, 1] - K, 0)   ❷

In [25]: C1   ❷
Out[25]: array([10,  5,  0,  0,  0])
```

```
In [26]: phi = np.linalg.solve(M, C1)   ❸

In [27]: phi   ❸
Out[27]: array([ 0.,   0.5,   0.01667, -0.2, -0.1])

In [28]: np.allclose(C1, np.dot(M, phi))   ❹
Out[28]: True

In [29]: C0 = np.dot(M0, phi)   ❺

In [30]: C0   ❺
Out[30]: 2.1666666666666665
```

❶ The strike price of the European call option, and the payoff vector of the relevant financial asset.

❷ The call option is written on the second traded financial asset with future payoff of $S_1^2 = (25, 20, 10, 5, 0)$.

❸ This solves the replication problem given the market payoff matrix.

❹ Checks whether the replication portfolio indeed replicates the future payoff of the European call option.

❺ From the replication portfolio, the arbitrage price follows in combination with the current price vector of the traded financial assets.

Market Completeness

Market completeness of the static model economy can be analyzed based on the *rank* of the market payoff matrix $\mathcal{M}$ as defined by the traded financial assets $\mathcal{S}$. The rank of a matrix equals the number of linearly independent (column) vectors (see Aleskerov et al. (2011), section 2.7). Consider the column vectors that represent the future price vectors of the traded financial assets. They are *linearly independent* if

$$\mathcal{M} \cdot \phi = 0$$

has only one solution, namely the null vector $\phi = (0, 0, \ldots, 0)^T \in \mathbb{R}^K$.

On the other hand, the *span* of the market payoff matrix $\mathcal{M}$ is given by all linear combinations of the column vectors:

$$\text{span}(\mathcal{M}) = \left\{ \phi \in \mathbb{R}^K : \mathcal{M} \cdot \phi \right\}$$

The model economy $\mathcal{E}$ is complete if the set of attainable contingent claims satisfies $\mathbb{A} = \mathbb{R}^I$. However, the set of attainable contingent claims equals by definition the span of the traded financial assets $\mathbb{A} \equiv \text{span}(\mathcal{M})$. The model economy $\mathcal{E}$ therefore is *complete* if:

$$\text{span}(\mathcal{M}) = \mathbb{R}^I$$

Under which circumstances is this the case? It is the case if the rank of the matrix is at least as large as the number of future states possible:

$$\text{rank}(\mathcal{M}) \geq I$$

In other words, the column vectors of $\mathcal{M}$ form a *basis* of the vector space $\mathbb{R}^I$ (with potentially more basis vectors than required). A *vector space* $\mathbb{V}$ is a set of elements (called *vectors*) that is characterized by:

1. An addition function mapping two vectors $v_1, v_2 \in \mathbb{V}$ to another element of the vector space $(v_1 + v_2) \in \mathbb{V}$.

2. A scalar multiplication function mapping a scalar $\alpha \in \mathbb{R}$ and a vector $v \in \mathbb{V}$ to another element of the vector space $(\alpha \cdot v) \in \mathbb{V}$.

3. A special element—usually called "zero" or "neutral element"—$0 \in \mathbb{V}$ such that $v + 0 = v$.

It is easy to verify that, for example, the sets $\mathbb{R}, \mathbb{R}^5$, or $\mathbb{R}^I, I \in \mathbb{N}_{>0}$ are vector spaces.

Consequently, the model economy is *incomplete* if:

$$\text{rank}(\mathcal{M}) < I$$

To make things a bit more concrete, consider a state space with three possible future states only, $\Omega = \{\omega_1, \omega_2, \omega_3\}$. All random variables, then, are vectors in the vector space $\mathbb{R}^3$. The following market payoff matrix—resulting from three traded financial assets—has a rank of 2 only because two-column vectors are linearly dependent. This leads to an incomplete market:

$$\mathcal{M} = \begin{pmatrix} 11 & 20 & 10 \\ 11 & 10 & 5 \\ 11 & 5 & 2.5 \end{pmatrix} \Rightarrow \text{rank}(\mathcal{M}) = 2$$

It is easily verified that the financial assets 2 and 3 are indeed linearly dependent:

$$S_1^2 = \begin{pmatrix} 20 \\ 10 \\ 5 \end{pmatrix} = 2 \cdot \begin{pmatrix} 10 \\ 5 \\ 2.5 \end{pmatrix} = 2 \cdot S_1^3$$

By contrast, the market payoff matrix that follows—resulting from a different set of three traded financial assets—has a rank of 3, leading to a complete market. In such a case, one also speaks of the matrix having *full rank*:

$$\mathcal{M} = \begin{pmatrix} 11 & 20 & 10 \\ 11 & 10 & 25 \\ 11 & 5 & 10 \end{pmatrix} \Rightarrow \text{rank}(\mathcal{M}) = 3$$

Assume next that a probability space is fixed for which the state space has five elements, $\Omega = \{\omega_1, \ldots, \omega_5\}$. The future (uncertain) price and payoff vectors of the five traded financial assets $\mathcal{S}$ and all contingent claims, respectively, are now elements of the vector space $\mathbb{R}^5$. The Python code that follows analyzes contingent claim replication based on such a model economy $\mathcal{E}$. It starts by assuming that all five Arrow-Debreu securities are traded and then proceeds to a randomized market payoff matrix:

```
In [31]: M = np.eye(5)   ❶

In [32]: M   ❶
Out[32]: array([[1., 0., 0., 0., 0.],
               [0., 1., 0., 0., 0.],
               [0., 0., 1., 0., 0.],
               [0., 0., 0., 1., 0.],
               [0., 0., 0., 0., 1.]])

In [33]: np.linalg.linalg.matrix_rank(M)   ❷
Out[33]: 5

In [34]: C1 = np.arange(10, 0, -2)   ❸

In [35]: C1   ❸
Out[35]: array([10,  8,  6,  4,  2])

In [36]: np.linalg.solve(M, C1)   ❹
Out[36]: array([10.,  8.,  6.,  4.,  2.])
```

❶ Creates a two-dimensional `ndarray` object, here an identity matrix. It can be interpreted as the market payoff matrix resulting from five traded Arrow-Debreu securities. It forms a so-called *canonical* basis of the vector space $\mathbb{R}^5$.

❷ Calculates the rank of the matrix, which is also trivial to see for the identity matrix.

❸ A contingent claim payoff that is to be replicated by the traded financial assets.

❹ This solves the replication (representation) problem, which is again trivial in the case of the identity matrix.

Next, a randomized market payoff matrix is generated, which happens to be of full rank as well (no guarantees here in general):

```
In [37]: rng = default_rng(100)   ❶

In [38]: M = rng.integers(1, 10, (5, 5))   ❷

In [39]: M   ❷
Out[39]: array([[7, 8, 2, 6, 1],
                [3, 4, 1, 6, 9],
                [9, 6, 4, 8, 9],
                [9, 1, 7, 7, 2],
                [5, 9, 7, 3, 3]])

In [40]: np.linalg.matrix_rank(M)   ❸
Out[40]: 5

In [41]: np.linalg.matrix_rank(M.T)   ❸
Out[41]: 5

In [42]: phi = np.linalg.solve(M, C1)   ❹

In [43]: phi   ❹
Out[43]: array([-1.16988,  0.52471, -0.3861 ,  2.56409, -0.62085])

In [44]: np.dot(M, phi)   ❺
Out[44]: array([10.,  8.,  6.,  4.,  2.])
```

❶ Fixes the seed for the `NumPy` random number generator, which allows for reproducibility of the results.

❷ Creates a randomized market payoff matrix (`ndarray` object with shape `(5, 5)` populated by random integers between 1 and 10).

❸ The matrix has full rank—both the column and row vectors are linearly independent.

❹ The nontrivial solution to the replication problem with the randomized basis for the vector space $\mathbb{R}^5$.

❺ Checks the solution for achieving perfect replication.

Fundamental Theorems of Asset Pricing

Consider the general static model economy $\mathscr{E} = (\{\Omega, \mathscr{F}, P\}, \mathscr{S})$, with I possible states and K traded financial assets. Assume that the risk-less short rate for lending and borrowing in the economy is $r \in \mathbb{R}_{\geq 0}$.[1]

An *arbitrage opportunity* is a portfolio $\phi \in \mathbb{R}^K$ of the traded financial assets $\mathscr{S}$ such that the price of the portfolio is zero

$$S_0 \cdot \phi = \sum_{k=1}^{K} S_0^k \cdot \phi^k = 0$$

and the expected payoff is greater than zero:

$$\mathbf{E}^P(\mathscr{M} \cdot \phi) > 0$$

Denote the *set of all arbitrage opportunities* by:

$$\mathbb{O} \equiv \left\{ \phi \in \mathbb{R}^K : S_0 \cdot \phi = 0, \mathbf{E}^P(\mathscr{M} \cdot \phi) > 0 \right\}$$

A *martingale measure* Q for the model economy makes the discounted price processes martingales and therefore satisfies the following condition:

$$\frac{1}{1+r} \cdot \mathbf{E}^Q(\mathscr{M}) = S_0$$

With these definitions, the *First Fundamental Theorem of Asset Pricing* (see also Chapter 2), which relates the existence of a martingale measure to the absence of arbitrage opportunities, can be formulated. For a discussion and proof, refer to Pliska (1997, section 1.3).

---

1 The notation is changed here from i to r to emphasize that the *short rate* is meant from now on.

First Fundamental Theorem of Asset Pricing (1FTAP)
The following statements are equivalent:

1. A martingale measure Q exists.

2. The economy is arbitrage-free, it holds $\mathbb{O} = \emptyset$.

The derivation of a martingale measure is formally the same as the solution of a replication problem for a contingent claim $C = (C_0, C_1)$, which reads

$$\mathcal{M} \cdot \phi = C_1$$

and where the replication portfolio ϕ needs to be determined. Mathematically, this is equivalent to solving a system of linear equations, as illustrated in Chapter 2. Finding a martingale measure can be written as

$$\frac{1}{1+r} \cdot \mathbf{E}^Q(\mathcal{M}) = \frac{1}{1+r}\mathcal{M}^T \cdot Q = \widetilde{\mathcal{M}} \cdot Q = S_0$$

where $\widetilde{\mathcal{M}} \equiv \frac{1}{1+r}\mathcal{M}^T$ and where

$$Q = \begin{pmatrix} Q(\omega_1) \\ Q(\omega_2) \\ \ldots \\ Q(\omega_I) \end{pmatrix}, \forall \omega \in \Omega : 0 \leq Q(\omega) \leq 1, \sum_{\omega \in \Omega} Q(\omega) = 1$$

This problem can be considered the *dual problem* to the replication problem—albeit under some restrictive constraints. The constraints, resulting from the requirement that the solution be a probability measure, make a different technical approach in Python necessary. The problem of finding a martingale measure can be modeled as a constrained minimization problem—instead of just solving a system of linear equation. The example assumes a state space with five elements and the market payoff structure from before:

```
In [45]: import scipy.optimize as sco      ❶

In [46]: M = np.array((
             (11, 25, 0,  0,  25),
             (11, 20, 30, 15, 25),
             (11, 10, 0,  20, 10),
             (11, 5,  30, 15, 0),
             (11, 0,  0,  0,  0)
         ))      ❷
```

```
In [47]: np.linalg.matrix_rank(M)  ❸
Out[47]: 5

In [48]: M0 = np.ones(5) * 10  ❹

In [49]: M0  ❺
Out[49]: array([10., 10., 10., 10., 10.])

In [50]: r = 0.1  ❻

In [51]: def E(Q):
             return np.sum((np.dot(M.T, Q) - M0 * (1 + r)) ** 2)  ❼

In [52]: E(np.array(5 * [0.2]))
Out[52]: 4.0

In [53]: cons = ({'type': 'eq', 'fun': lambda Q: Q.sum() - 1})  ❽

In [54]: bnds = (5 * [(0, 1)])  ❾

In [55]: bnds  ❾
Out[55]: [(0, 1), (0, 1), (0, 1), (0, 1), (0, 1)]

In [56]: res = sco.minimize(E, 5 * [1],  ❿
                           method='SLSQP',  ⓫
                           constraints=cons,  ⓬
                           bounds=bnds)  ⓭

In [57]: Q = res['x']  ⓮

In [58]: Q  ⓮
Out[58]: array([0.14667, 0.18333, 0.275  , 0.18333, 0.21167])

In [59]: np.dot(M.T, Q) / (1 + r)  ⓯
Out[59]: array([10.    , 9.99998, 9.99999, 10.00001, 9.99998])

In [60]: np.allclose(M0, np.dot(M.T, Q) / (1 + r))
Out[60]: True
```

❶ Imports the optimize subpackage from scipy as sco.

❷ Defines the market payoff matrix.

❸ Verifies that the matrix is of full rank.

❹ Defines the price vector for the traded financial assets…

❺ …and shows the values, which are all set to 10.

❻ Fixes the constant short rate.

❼ Defines the objective function that is to be minimized. This approach is necessary because the linear system is to be solved under a constraint and with bounds for all parameters.

❽ The constraint that the single probabilities need to add up to one.

❾ Defines the bounds for every single probability.

❿ The optimization procedure minimizing the function E…

⓫ …defining the method used,…

⓬ …providing the constraints to be observed, and…

⓭ …providing the bounds for the parameters.

⓮ The results vector is the martingale measure.

⓯ Under the martingale measure, the discounted price processes are martingales.

The second Fundamental Theorem of Asset Pricing also holds true in the general static model economy $\mathcal{E}$. For a discussion and proof, refer to Pliska (1997, section 1.5).

Second Fundamental Theorem of Asset Pricing (2FTAP)
The following statements are equivalent:

1. The martingale measure Q is unique.

2. The economy is complete, it holds $\mathbb{A} = \mathbb{R}_+^I$.

Fundamental Theorems

The quest for valid option pricing models led to the seminal option pricing models of Black and Scholes (1973) and Merton (1973)—together Black-Scholes-Merton (1973). The models used in these seminal papers are rather specific in that they assume a geometric Brownian motion as the model for the price process of the only risky asset. Research from the late 1970s and early 1980s, namely from Harrison and Kreps (1979) and Harrison and Pliska (1981), provides a general framework for the pricing of contingent claims. In their general framework, martingale measures and processes that are (semi-)martingales play the central role. The class of (semi-)martingale processes is pretty large and encompasses both the early models (for example, geometric Brownian motion) as well as many more sophisticated financial models proposed and analyzed much later (for example, jump diffusions or stochastic volatility processes). Among others, this is one of the reasons why the presented theorems are called *fundamental*—they apply to a large class of interesting and important financial models.

Black-Scholes-Merton Option Pricing

The Black-Scholes-Merton (1973) model for option pricing is based on a continuous model economy generally represented by stochastic differential equations (SDEs) with suitable boundary conditions. The SDE used to describe the evolution of the *single risky asset* (think of a stock or stock index) is the one for a *geometric Brownian motion*. In addition to the risky asset, another *risk-less asset* is traded in their model economy and it pays a continuous, risk-less short rate.

In the static case with two relevant points in time only, say $t = 0$ and $t = T > 0$, the future, uncertain value of the risky asset S_T is given by

$$S_T = S_0 \cdot e^{\left(r - \frac{\sigma^2}{2}\right)T + \sigma\sqrt{T}z}$$

where $S_0 \in \mathbb{R}_{>0}$ is the price of the risky asset today, $r \in \mathbb{R}_{\geq 0}$ is the constant risk-less short rate, $\sigma \in \mathbb{R}_{>0}$ is a constant volatility factor, and z is a standard normally distributed random variable (see Jacod and Protter (2004), chapter 16).

In a discrete, numerical context, one can draw, for example, pseudo-random numbers $z_i, i = 1, 2, \ldots, I$ that are standard normally distributed to derive I numerical values for S_T according to the preceding equation:

$$S_T(z_i) = S_0 \cdot e^{\left(r - \frac{\sigma^2}{2}\right)T + \sigma\sqrt{T}z_i}, i = 1, 2, \ldots, I$$

Such a procedure is usually called a *Monte Carlo simulation*. To simplify the notation, S_T shall from now on specify the vector of simulated future values of the stock:

$$S_T \equiv \begin{pmatrix} S_T(z_1) \\ S_T(z_2) \\ \ldots \\ S_T(z_I) \end{pmatrix}$$

With these definitions, the model economy is as follows. There is a general probability space $\{\Omega, \mathscr{F} \equiv \wp(\Omega), P\}$ with I possible future states of the economy. Every state is assumed to be equally likely—that is, it holds:

$$\forall \omega \in \Omega: P(\omega) = \frac{1}{I}$$

The set of traded financial assets $\mathscr{S}$ consists of the risk-less asset called *bond* with price process $B = \left(B_0, B_0 \cdot e^{rT}\right)$ and the risky asset called *stock* (paying no dividends) with price process $S = \left(S_0, S_T\right)$ and S_T as defined previously. Together this forms the Black-Scholes-Merton (1973) model economy:

$$\mathscr{E}^{BSM} = (\{\Omega, \mathscr{F}, P\}, \mathscr{S} = \{B, S\})$$

Assume a European call option written on the stock as a contingent claim. The payoff is

$$C_T \equiv \left(S_T - K, 0\right)$$

with strike price $K \in \mathbb{R}_{\geq 0}$. The price—here, the *Monte Carlo estimator*—for the call option is given as the expected (average) discounted payoff:

$$C_0 = e^{-rT} \frac{1}{I} \sum_{i=1}^{I} \max\left(S_T(z_i) - K, 0\right)$$

The model economy and the Monte Carlo–based pricing approach are straightforward to implement in Python. Figure 5-1 shows the frequency distribution of the simulated stock price values, including the mean and the standard deviation around the mean:

```
In [61]: import math

In [62]: S0 = 100    ❶
         r = 0.05    ❷
         sigma = 0.2    ❸
         T = 1.0    ❹
         I = 10000    ❺

In [63]: rng = default_rng(100)    ❻

In [64]: ST = S0 * np.exp((r - sigma ** 2 / 2) * T +
                sigma * math.sqrt(T) * rng.standard_normal(I))    ❼

In [65]: ST[:8].round(1)    ❼
Out[65]: array([ 81.7, 109.2, 120.5, 114.9,  85. , 127.7, 118.6, 118.6])

In [66]: ST.mean()    ❽
Out[66]: 105.6675325917807

In [67]: S0 * math.exp(r * T)    ❾
Out[67]: 105.12710963760242

In [68]: from pylab import mpl, plt
         plt.style.use('seaborn')
         mpl.rcParams['savefig.dpi'] = 300
         mpl.rcParams['font.family'] = 'serif'

In [69]: plt.figure(figsize=(10, 6))
         plt.hist(ST, bins=35, label='frequency');
         plt.axvline(ST.mean(), color='r', label='mean')
         plt.axvline(ST.mean() + ST.std(), color='y', label='sd up')
         plt.axvline(ST.mean() - ST.std(), color='y', label='sd down')
         plt.legend(loc=0);    ❿
```

❶ The initial stock price level.

❷ The constant short rate.

❸ The volatility factor.

❹ The time horizon in year fractions.

❺ The number of states and also the number of simulations.

❻ Fixes the seed value for reproducibility.

❼ The core line of code: it implements the Monte Carlo simulation with NumPy in vectorized fashion, simulating I values in a single step.

❽ The mean value as obtained from the simulated set of stock prices.

❾ The theoretically to-be-expected value of the stock price.

❿ These lines of code plot the simulation results as a histogram and add some major statistics.

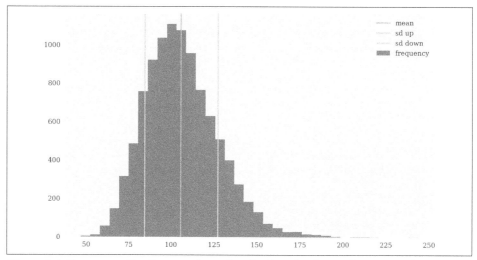

Figure 5-1. Frequency distribution of simulated values for the stock price in Black-Scholes-Merton (1973)

Having the simulated stock price values available makes European option pricing only a matter of two more vectorized operations:

```
In [70]: K = 105  ❶

In [71]: CT = np.maximum(ST - K, 0)  ❷

In [72]: CT[:8].round(1)
Out[72]: array([ 0. ,  4.2, 15.5,  9.9,  0. , 22.7, 13.6, 13.6])

In [73]: C0 = math.exp(-r * T) * CT.mean()  ❸

In [74]: C0  ❸
Out[74]: 8.288763195530931
```

❶ The strike price of the option.

❷ The payoff vector of the option.

❸ The Monte Carlo estimator of the option price.

Completeness of Black-Scholes-Merton

What about the completeness of the Black-Scholes-Merton model economy $\mathcal{E}^{BSM}$?
The previous section derives a Monte Carlo estimator for the (arbitrage) price of a
European call option despite the fact that there are many more states of the economy,
$I \gg 2$, than financial assets traded, $K = 2$. Two observations can be made:

General incompleteness
> In a wider sense, the economy is incomplete because not every contingent claim
> can be replicated by a portfolio of the traded assets and because there is not a
> unique martingale measure (see 2FTAP).

Specific completeness
> In a narrow sense, the model is complete, because every contingent claim that
> can be represented as a function of the price vector of the stock $C_1 = f\left(S_1^2\right)$ is rep-
> licable by positions in the bond and the stock.

When using Monte Carlo simulation to derive an estimator for the arbitrage price in
the previous section, the fact is used that the model economy $\mathcal{E}^{BSM}$ is complete in the
previous specific, narrow sense. The payoff of the European call option only depends
on the future price vector of the stock. What is missing so far is the replication portfolio and the resulting arbitrage price calculation to verify that the Monte Carlo simulation approach is justified.

The NumPy function used so far to solve replication problems, np.linalg.solve,
requires a square (market payoff) matrix. In the Black-Scholes-Merton economy with
only two traded financial assets and many more possible future states, this prerequisite is not given. However, one can use a least-squares approach via np.linalg.lstsq
to find a numerical solution to the replication problem:

```
In [75]: B0 = 100   ❶

In [76]: M0 = np.array((B0, S0))   ❷

In [77]: BT = B0 * np.ones(len(ST)) * math.exp(r * T)   ❸

In [78]: BT[:4]   ❸
Out[78]: array([105.12711, 105.12711, 105.12711, 105.12711])
```

```
In [79]: M = np.array((BT, ST)).T  ❹

In [80]: M  ❹
Out[80]: array([[105.12711,  81.74955],
                [105.12711, 109.19348],
                [105.12711, 120.4628 ],
                ...,
                [105.12711,  71.10624],
                [105.12711, 105.32038],
                [105.12711, 134.77647]])

In [81]: phi = np.linalg.lstsq(M, CT, rcond=None)[0]  ❺

In [82]: phi  ❺
Out[82]: array([-0.51089,  0.59075])

In [83]: np.mean((np.dot(M, phi) - CT))  ❻
Out[83]: 1.1798206855928583e-14

In [84]: np.dot(M0, phi)  ❼
Out[84]: 7.9850808951857335
```

❶ The arbitrarily fixed price for the bond.

❷ The price vector today for the two traded financial assets.

❸ The future price vector of the bond given the initial price and the short rate.

❹ The resulting market payoff matrix, which is of rank 2 only—compared to 10,000 future states.

❺ This solves the replication problem through least-squares representation. For the call option replication, the bond is to be shorted (sold), and the stock is to be bought.

❻ The average replication error, resulting, for example, from floating point inaccuracies and the numerical methods used, is not exactly zero but really close to it.

❼ This calculates the arbitrage price given the (numerically) optimal replication portfolio. It is close to the Monte Carlo estimator from before.

Merton Jump-Diffusion Option Pricing

This section introduces another important model economy that dates back to Merton (1976) and adds a jump component to the stock price model of Black-Scholes-Merton (1973). The random jump component renders the model economy $\mathcal{M}^{M76}$ incomplete in general. However, in the discrete setting of this chapter, one can apply the same numerical approaches for option pricing as introduced for $\mathcal{E}^{BSM}$ in the previous two sections. The model is called the *jump-diffusion* model, although a diffusion is only defined in a dynamic context.

In real financial time series, one observes jumps with some regularities. They might be caused by a stock market crash or by other rare and/or extreme events. The model by Merton (1976) allows us to explicitly model such rare events and their impact on the price of financial instruments. Models without jumps are often not well suited to explain certain characteristics and phenomena as regularly observed in financial time series. The model is also capable of modeling both positive and negative jumps. While a negative jump (large drop) might be observed in practice for stock indices, positive jumps (spikes) occur in practice, for example, in volatility indices.

The *Merton jump-diffusion economy* $\mathcal{E}^{M76}$ is the same as the Black-Scholes-Merton economy $\mathcal{E}^{BSM}$ apart from the future price of the stock at time T, which can be simulated in this economy according to

$$S_T(z_i) = S_0 \cdot \left(e^{\left(r - r_j - \frac{\sigma^2}{2} \right) T + \sigma \sqrt{T} z_i^1 +} + \left(e^{\mu + \delta z_i^2} - 1 \right) y_i \right), i = 1, 2, \ldots, I$$

with the z_i^1, z_i^2 being standard normally distributed and the y_i being Poisson distributed with intensity λ (see Jacod and Protter (2004), chapter 4). The jumps are lognormally distributed with an expected value of μ and standard deviation of δ (see Jacod and Protter (2004), chapter 7). The expected jump size is:

$$r_j = \lambda \cdot \left(e^{\mu + \delta^2/2} - 1 \right)$$

Implementing and simulating this model in Python requires the definition of additional parameters and the simulation of three random variables. Figure 5-2 shows the frequency distribution of the simulated values, which can become negative given the parameters assumed and the Python code used:

```
In [85]: M0 = np.array((100, 100))    ❶

In [86]: r = 0.05
         sigma = 0.2
         lmbda = 0.3
         mu = -0.3
         delta = 0.1
         rj = lmbda * (math.exp(mu + delta ** 2 / 2) - 1)
         T = 1.0
```

```
           I = 10000

In [87]: BT = M0[0] * np.ones(I) * math.exp(r * T)

In [88]: z = rng.standard_normal((2, I))  ❷
         z -= z.mean()  ❸
         z /= z.std()  ❸
         y = rng.poisson(lmbda, I)  ❹

In [89]: ST = S0 * (
             np.exp((r - rj - sigma ** 2 / 2) * T +
                 sigma * math.sqrt(T) * z[0]) +
             (np.exp(mu + delta * z[1]) - 1) * y
         )  ❺

In [90]: ST.mean() * math.exp(-r * T)  ❻
Out[90]: 100.53765025420363

In [91]: plt.figure(figsize=(10, 6))
         plt.hist(ST, bins=35, label='frequency');
         plt.axvline(ST.mean(), color='r', label='mean')
         plt.axvline(ST.mean() + ST.std(), color='y', label='sd up')
         plt.axvline(ST.mean() - ST.std(), color='y', label='sd down')
         plt.legend(loc=0);
```

❶ Fixes the initial price vector of the two traded financial assets (bond and stock).

❷ The first set of standard normally distributed random numbers.

❸ The second set of standard normally distributed random numbers.

❹ The set with Poisson distributed random numbers with intensity lambda.

❺ The simulation of the stock price values at T given the three sets of random numbers.

❻ Calculates the discounted mean value of the simulated stock price.

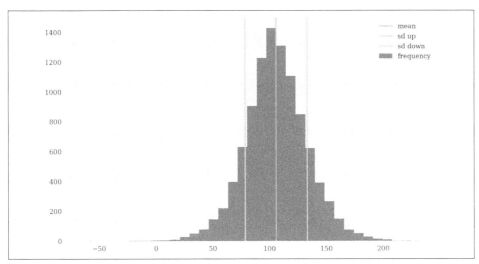

Figure 5-2. Frequency distribution of the simulated values for the stock price in Merton (1976)

Adding a maximum function to the stock price, Monte Carlo simulation avoids negative values (see Figure 5-3):

```
In [92]: ST = np.maximum(S0 * (
             np.exp((r - rj - sigma ** 2 / 2) * T +
                 sigma * math.sqrt(T) * z[0]) +
             (np.exp(mu + delta * z[1]) - 1) * y
         ), 0)  ❶
```

```
In [93]: plt.figure(figsize=(10, 6))
         plt.hist(ST, bins=35, label='frequency')  ❷
         plt.axvline(ST.mean(), color='r', label='mean')
         plt.axvline(ST.mean() + ST.std(), color='y', label='sd up')
         plt.axvline(ST.mean() - ST.std(), color='y', label='sd down')
         plt.legend(loc=0);
```

❶ Maximum function…

❷ …avoids negative values for the stock price.

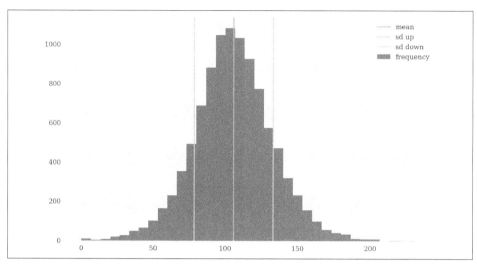

Figure 5-3. Simulated values (truncated) for the stock price in Merton (1976)

The final step is the pricing of the European call option through calculation of the Monte Carlo estimator and the approximate replication approach:

```
In [94]: K = 105

In [95]: CT = np.maximum(ST - K, 0)

In [96]: C0 = math.exp(-r * T)  * np.mean(CT)  ❶

In [97]: C0  ❶
Out[97]: 10.306374338651601

In [98]: M = np.array((BT, ST)).T

In [99]: phi = np.linalg.lstsq(M, CT, rcond=-1)[0]  ❷

In [100]: phi  ❷
Out[100]: array([-0.41827,  0.51847])

In [101]: np.mean(np.dot(M, phi) - CT)  ❸
Out[101]: 1.1823431123048067e-15

In [102]: np.dot(M0, phi)  ❹
Out[102]: 10.020157308565008
```

❶ The Monte Carlo estimator for the European call option price.

❷ The approximate replication portfolio.

❸ The replication error of the optimal portfolio.

❹ The arbitrage price according to the optimal portfolio.

Incompleteness Through Jumps

While the Black-Scholes-Merton (1973) model is complete in a narrow sense, the addition of a jump component in the Merton (1976) jump diffusion model makes it incomplete in a wide sense. This means that even the introduction of additional financial assets cannot make it complete. The fact that the jump component can take on an infinite number of values would require an infinite number of additional financial assets to make the model complete.

Representative Agent Pricing

Assume again the general static economy $\mathscr{E}$ now populated by a *representative, expected utility maximizing agent*. The agent is endowed with initial wealth today of $w \in \mathbb{R}_{>0}$ and has preferences that can be represented by a utility function $u : c \to \mathbb{R}, u(c) \mapsto \ln c$. Formally, the problem of the agent is the same as in Chapter 4:

$$\max_{\phi} \ \mathbf{E}^{P}(u(\mathscr{M} \cdot \phi))$$
$$w \ = \ \mathscr{M}_0 \cdot \phi$$

The difference is that there are now potentially many more future states possible and many more financial assets traded.

Furthermore, assuming that the complete set of Arrow-Debreu securities—with a net supply of one for each security—is traded, $K = I$, the *market payoff matrix* is:

$$\mathscr{M} = \begin{pmatrix} 1 & 0 & \dots & 0 \\ 0 & 1 & \dots & 0 \\ \multicolumn{4}{c}{\dots\dots\dots\dots} \\ 0 & 0 & \dots & 1 \end{pmatrix}$$

The optimization problem in unconstrained form is according to the Theorem of Lagrange given by:

$$\max_{\phi, \lambda} \ f(\phi, \lambda) = \mathbf{E}^{P}(u(\mathscr{M} \cdot \phi)) - \lambda \cdot (\mathscr{M}_0 \cdot \phi - w)$$

From this, the first-order conditions for all portfolio positions ϕ_i, $i = 1, 2, \ldots, I$—where i refers to the Arrow-Debreu security that pays off in state ω_i—are:

$$\frac{\partial f}{\partial \phi_i} = P(\omega_i) - \lambda \cdot S_0^i = 0, i = 1, 2, \ldots, I$$

S_0^i is the price of the Arrow-Debreu security paying off in state ω_i. The relative prices between all Arrow-Debreu securities are accordingly determined by the probabilities for the respective payoff states to unfold:

$$\frac{S_0^i}{S_0^j} = \frac{P(\omega_i)}{P(\omega_j)}, \omega_i, \omega_j \in \Omega$$

Fixing $w = 1$, one obtains for the absolute prices:

$$S_0^i = P(\omega_i)$$

In words, the price for the Arrow-Debreu security paying off in state ω_i equals the probability $P(\omega_i)$ for this state to unfold.

This little analysis shows that the formalism of solving the representative agent problem for pricing purposes is more or less the same in the general static economy as compared to the simple economies of Chapter 4.

Conclusions

This chapter covers *general static economies* with a potentially large number of states —for the Black-Scholes-Merton (1973) model simulation, for example, 10,000 different states are assumed. The additional formalism introduced pays off pretty well because it allows for much more realistic models that can be applied in practice, for instance, to value European put or call options on a stock index or a single stock.

Python in combination with NumPy proves powerful for the modeling of such economies with much larger market payoff matrices than seen before. Monte Carlo simulation is also accomplished both efficiently and quickly by the use of vectorization techniques. Using least-squares regression techniques, approximate replication portfolios are efficiently derived in such a setting.

However, static economies are limited per se with regard to what they can model in the financial space. For instance, early exercise features like those seen in the context of American options cannot be accounted for. This shortcoming will be overcome when enlarging the relevant set of points in time—making thereby the next natural step to dynamic economies—in the next chapter.

Further Resources

Papers cited in this chapter:

Black, Fischer and Myron Scholes. 1973. "The Pricing of Options and Corporate Liabilities." *Journal of Political Economy* 81 (3): 638–659.

Harrison, Michael and David Kreps. 1979. "Martingales and Arbitrage in Multiperiod Securities Markets." *Journal of Economic Theory* (20): 381–408.

Harrison, Michael and Stanley Pliska. 1981. "Martingales and Stochastic Integrals in the Theory of Continuous Trading." *Stochastic Processes and their Applications* (11): 215–260.

Merton, Robert. 1973. "Theory of Rational Option Pricing." *Bell Journal of Economics and Management Science* (4): 141–183.

Merton, Robert. 1976. "Option Pricing when the Underlying Stock Returns are Discontinuous." *Journal of Financial Economics* 3 (3): 125–144.

Books cited in this chapter:

Aleskerov, Fuad, Hasan Ersel, and Dmitri Piontkovski. 2011. *Linear Algebra for Economists*. Heidelberg: Springer.

Delbaen, Freddy and Walter Schachermayer. 2006. *The Mathematics of Arbitrage*. Berlin: Springer Verlag.

Duffie, Darrell. 1988. *Security Markets—Stochastic Models*. San Diego: Academic Press.

Jacod, Jean and Philip Protter. 2004. *Probability Essentials*. Berlin and Heidelberg: Springer.

Milne, Frank. 1995. *Finance Theory and Asset Pricing*. New York: Oxford University Press.

Pliska, Stanley. 1997. *Introduction to Mathematical Finance*. Malden and Oxford: Blackwell Publishers.

## CHAPTER 6

Dynamic Economy

Multiperiod models of securities markets are much more realistic than single period models. In fact, they are extensively used for practical purposes in the financial industry.

—Stanley Pliska (1997)

Although markets are not complete at any one time, they are dynamically complete in the sense that any consumption process can be financed by trading the given set of financial securities, adjusting portfolios through time as uncertainty is resolved bit by bit.

—Darrell Duffie (1986)

In reality, quantitative information—such as changes in stock prices or interest rates —is revealed gradually over time. While static model economies are an elegant way of introducing fundamental notions in finance, a realistic financial model requires a dynamic representation of the financial world.

The formalism needed to properly model dynamic economies is more involved and cannot be covered in full detail in this chapter. However, the chapter can present two of the most important dynamic model economies based on discrete time dynamics: the Cox-Ross-Rubinstein (1979) binomial option pricing model and the Black-Scholes-Merton (1973) option pricing model in a discrete Monte Carlo simulation version. In this context, *discrete time* means that the set of relevant dates is extended from just two to a larger, but still finite, number—say, to five or 50.

The tools used in this chapter are more or less the same as before: linear algebra, probability theory, and also, like in the previous chapter, stochastic elements to implement Monte Carlo simulation. Duffie (1988) and Pliska (1997) are great resources for dynamic financial modeling in discrete time. Glasserman (2004) is a comprehensive reference book for Monte Carlo simulation methods in finance.

Topics covered in this chapter are stochastic processes, option pricing in dynamically complete markets, binomial option pricing, Black-Scholes-Merton (1973) dynamic simulation, early exercise and American option pricing, as well as Least-Squares Monte Carlo (LSM) option pricing.

The following table gives an overview of the topics in finance, mathematics, and Python found in this chapter:

Finance	Mathematics	Python
Uncertainty, tree-based	Stochastic process, binomial tree	`NumPy, ndarray`
Uncertainty, simulation-based	Stochastic process, Monte Carlo simulation	`NumPy, ndarray, rng.standard_normal`
European option pricing	Inner values, backward induction, risk-neutral expectation	`NumPy, ndarray, np.maximum`
American option pricing	Inner values, continuation values, OLS regression, backward induction, risk-neutral expectation	`NumPy, ndarray, np.polyval, np.polyfit, np.where`

As in Chapter 5, the major goal of this chapter is *generalization*. While Chapter 5 generalizes the *state space*, this chapter sets out to generalize the *discrete set of relevant points in time* at which new information is revealed and economic action takes place. While some additional formalism is needed to do so, the chapter is, on the other hand, less formal since it focuses on two specific models only and does not try to provide a general framework for dynamic economies in discrete time. Such a general framework, including many examples implemented in Python, is found in Hilpisch (2015).

Binomial Option Pricing

The binomial option pricing model became popular immediately after publication in 1979—both as a numerically efficient method to price European options and American options as well as a teaching tool. While the Black-Scholes-Merton (1973) model relies on continuous time finance and stochastic calculus, the binomial option pricing model is, in a sense, a discrete time version of the BSM model that can be fully understood with elementary mathematics only.

In the Cox-Ross-Rubinstein (1979) model, there are two traded financial assets: a risky one, called *stock*, and a risk-less one, called *bond*. The model economy is considered over a *finite set of dates* $\mathcal{T} \equiv \{t_0 = 0, t_1, t_2, \ldots, t_M = T\}$, with $M + 1, M > 1$ elements.

Given a stock price of S_{t_i}, the stock price at the next date $S_{t_{i+1}}$ can only take on two different values:

$$S_{t_{i+1}} = \begin{cases} S_{t_i} \cdot u \\ S_{t_i} \cdot d \end{cases}$$

u stands for an *upward movement* and d for a *downward movement*.

To simplify the handling of dates, assume an evenly spaced time grid with M time intervals of length $\Delta t = \frac{T}{M}$ each. The finite set of dates can then be written as $\mathcal{T} \equiv \{t_0 = 0, t_1 = \Delta t, t_2 = 2\Delta t, \ldots, T\}$. In addition, define:

$$\begin{cases} u \equiv e^{\sigma\sqrt{\Delta t}} \\ d \equiv e^{-\sigma\sqrt{\Delta t}} = u^{-1} \end{cases}$$

It turns out that one consequence of this definition is the property $u \cdot d = 1$, which will prove convenient in that it creates a so-called *recombining* binomial tree. $\sigma \in \mathbb{R}_{>0}$ represents the constant *volatility factor*.

Assume that the risk-less, constant short rate is given by $r \in \mathbb{R}_{\geq 0}$. Given a bond price of B_{t_i}, the price of the bond one period later is given by

$$B_{t_{i+1}} = B_{t_i} \cdot e^{r \cdot (t_{i+1} - t_i)}$$

or

$$B_{t+\Delta t} = B_t \cdot e^{r \cdot \Delta t}$$

for some $t \in \mathcal{T} \setminus T$.

A central numerical parameter value to be derived, based on the preceding assumptions, is the martingale probability for an upward movement at any given node. Given that there are only two branches for every node, the downward probability is then known as well. Denote the *martingale probability* for an upward movement by $q \in \mathbb{R}_{>0}, 0 < q < 1$. One gets from the martingale property for the stock price:

$$
\begin{aligned}
S_t &= \quad e^{-r\Delta t}\mathbf{E}^Q\!\left(S_{t+\Delta t}\right) \\
&= e^{-r\Delta t}\!\left(qS_t u + (1-q)S_t d\right) \\
\Longleftrightarrow 1 &= \quad e^{-r\Delta t}\!\left(qu + (1-q)d\right) \\
\Longleftrightarrow q &= \quad \frac{e^{r\Delta t} - d}{u - d}
\end{aligned}
$$

This shows that the martingale measure is fixed at every node and consequently for the whole tree.

The basics of the binomial option pricing model are easily translated into Python code:[1]

```
In [1]: import math
        import numpy as np

In [2]: S0 = 36.    ❶
        K = 40.     ❷
        r = 0.06    ❸
        T = 1.0     ❹
        sigma = 0.2 ❺

In [3]: m = 4       ❻
        dt = T / m  ❼
        df = math.exp(-r * dt)            ❽
        up = math.exp(sigma * math.sqrt(dt))  ❾
        down = 1 / up   ❾

In [4]: q = (1 / df - down) / (up - down)   ❿
```

❶ The initial stock price value.

❷ The strike price for the option to be valued.

❸ The constant risk-less short rate.

❹ The time horizon and option maturity.

❺ The constant volatility factor.

❻ The number of time intervals.

❼ The resulting length of each time interval.

---

1 The parameters assumed in this chapter are from Longstaff and Schwartz (2001, table 1).

❽ The discount factor for the fixed time interval.

❾ The upward and downward factors.

❿ The martingale probability for an upward movement.

The simulation of the stock price process and the valuation of options in this model are a bit more involved. The following presents two different implementations: one based on *Python loops*, which might be easier to understand at the beginning, and one based on *vectorized* NumPy *code*, which is more concise and efficient, but may be a bit harder to grasp at first.

Simulation and Valuation Based on Python Loops

Even though the implementation in this subsection uses Python loops, the basic data structure is a NumPy ndarray object:

```
In [5]: S = np.zeros((m + 1, m + 1))   ❶
        S   ❶
Out[5]: array([[0., 0., 0., 0., 0.],
               [0., 0., 0., 0., 0.],
               [0., 0., 0., 0., 0.],
               [0., 0., 0., 0., 0.],
               [0., 0., 0., 0., 0.]])

In [6]: S[0, 0] = S0   ❷
        S   ❷
Out[6]: array([[36.,  0.,  0.,  0.,  0.],
               [ 0.,  0.,  0.,  0.,  0.],
               [ 0.,  0.,  0.,  0.,  0.],
               [ 0.,  0.,  0.,  0.,  0.],
               [ 0.,  0.,  0.,  0.,  0.]])

In [7]: z = 1   ❸
        for t in range(1, m + 1):   ❹
            for i in range(0, z):   ❺
                S[i, t] = S[i, t - 1] * up   ❻
                S[i + 1 ,t] = S[i, t - 1] * down   ❻
            z += 1   ❼

In [8]: np.set_printoptions(formatter=
                {'float_kind': lambda x: '%7.3f' % x})

In [9]: S   ❽
Out[9]: array([[ 36.000,  39.786,  43.970,  48.595,  53.706],
               [  0.000,  32.574,  36.000,  39.786,  43.970],
               [  0.000,   0.000,  29.474,  32.574,  36.000],
               [  0.000,   0.000,   0.000,  26.669,  29.474],
               [  0.000,   0.000,   0.000,   0.000,  24.132]])
```

❶ Initializes the `ndarray` object.

❷ Sets the initial stock price value in the upper-lefthand corner.

❸ Sets a counter `z` to 1.

❹ Iterates from 1 to `m+1`, that is, over all time steps after 0.

❺ Iterates over the relevant nodes for the given time step.

❻ Calculates the up and down values and sets them in the `ndarray` object.

❼ Increases the counter by 1 to include more relevant nodes in the next step.

❽ The resulting recombining binomial tree.

European option pricing

The valuation of a European option based on the available stock price process happens by calculating the inner values of the option at maturity and applying *backward induction*. This basically means starting at the end, moving backward step by step to the present, and at every node repeatedly applying the risk-neutral pricing paradigm as introduced in the simple static two-state economy of Chapter 2.

The following Python code assumes a European put option payoff:

```
In [10]: h = np.zeros_like(S)   ❶

In [11]: z = 1
         for t in range(0, m + 1):
             for i in range(0, z):
                 h[i, t] = max(K - S[i, t], 0)   ❷
             z += 1

In [12]: h   ❷
Out[12]: array([[  4.000,   0.214,   0.000,   0.000,   0.000],
               [  0.000,   7.426,   4.000,   0.214,   0.000],
               [  0.000,   0.000,  10.526,   7.426,   4.000],
               [  0.000,   0.000,   0.000,  13.331,  10.526],
               [  0.000,   0.000,   0.000,   0.000,  15.868]])

In [13]: V = np.zeros_like(S)
         V[:, -1] = h[:, -1]
         V
Out[13]: array([[  0.000,   0.000,   0.000,   0.000,   0.000],
               [  0.000,   0.000,   0.000,   0.000,   0.000],
               [  0.000,   0.000,   0.000,   0.000,   4.000],
               [  0.000,   0.000,   0.000,   0.000,  10.526],
               [  0.000,   0.000,   0.000,   0.000,  15.868]])
```

```
In [14]: m
Out[14]: 4

In [15]: # European option pricing
         z = 0
         for t in range(m - 1, -1, -1):
             for i in range(0, m - z):
                 V[i, t] = df * (q * V[i, t + 1] +
                                 (1-q) * V[i + 1, t + 1])  ❸
             z += 1

In [16]: V  ❹
Out[16]: array([[  3.977,   2.190,   0.784,   0.000,   0.000],
                [  0.000,   6.299,   3.985,   1.771,   0.000],
                [  0.000,   0.000,   9.344,   6.830,   4.000],
                [  0.000,   0.000,   0.000,  12.735,  10.526],
                [  0.000,   0.000,   0.000,   0.000,  15.868]])

In [17]: V[0, 0]  ❺
Out[17]: 3.9771456941187893
```

❶ The ndarray object for the inner values.

❷ This calculates the inner values for the relevant nodes.

❸ This does the node-wise valuation by applying risk-neutral pricing.

❹ The resulting present value binomial tree.

❺ The present value today of the European put option.

American option pricing

One of the major features of the binomial option pricing model is that American options are as easily valued as their European counterparts. An *American option* can be exercised at any time *on and before* the maturity date. The adjustment to be made to the backward valuation algorithm is simple: one just needs to check whether the inner value of the American option is at any given node higher than the continuation value, that is, the present value of not exercising the option. If that is the case, the option is exercised, and the value of the American option is set to the inner value. Formally, one gets

$$V_t = \max\left[h_t, e^{-r\Delta t}\mathbf{E}^Q(V_{t+\Delta t})\right]$$

where h_t is the inner value at time t, and $e^{-r\Delta t}\mathbf{E}^Q(V_{t+\Delta t})$ is the continuation value.

In Python, a single line of code needs to be added:

```
In [18]: # American option pricing
         z = 0
         for t in range(m - 1, -1, -1):
             for i in range(0, m-z):
                 V[i, t] = df * (q * V[i, t + 1] +
                            (1 - q) * V[i + 1, t + 1])
                 V[i, t] = max(h[i, t], V[i, t])   ❶
             z += 1

In [19]: V   ❷
Out[19]: array([[  4.540,   2.307,   0.784,   0.000,   0.000],
                [  0.000,   7.426,   4.249,   1.771,   0.000],
                [  0.000,   0.000,  10.526,   7.426,   4.000],
                [  0.000,   0.000,   0.000,  13.331,  10.526],
                [  0.000,   0.000,   0.000,   0.000,  15.868]])

In [20]: V[0, 0]   ❸
Out[20]: 4.539560595224299
```

❶ This line checks for the early exercise decision and puts the inner value as the American option value when it is higher than the continuation value.

❷ The resulting binomial tree for the present values of the American put option.

❸ The present value today of the American put option, which is considerably higher than without early exercise.

Simulation and Valuation Based on Vectorized Code

The algorithm implementation that follows makes systematic use of NumPy vectorization capabilities. The implementation is presented step by step, also with some illustrating lines of code not needed for the algorithm implementation itself:

```
In [21]: u = np.arange(m + 1)   ❶
         u   ❶
Out[21]: array([0, 1, 2, 3, 4])

In [22]: u ** 2   ❷
Out[22]: array([ 0,  1,  4,  9, 16])

In [23]: 2 ** u   ❸
Out[23]: array([ 1,  2,  4,  8, 16])

In [24]: u = np.resize(u, (m + 1, m + 1))   ❹
         u
Out[24]: array([[0, 1, 2, 3, 4],
                [0, 1, 2, 3, 4],
                [0, 1, 2, 3, 4],
```

```
                [0, 1, 2, 3, 4],
                [0, 1, 2, 3, 4]])

In [25]: d = u.T  ❺
         d  ❺
Out[25]: array([[0, 0, 0, 0, 0],
                [1, 1, 1, 1, 1],
                [2, 2, 2, 2, 2],
                [3, 3, 3, 3, 3],
                [4, 4, 4, 4, 4]])

In [26]: (u - 2 * d)  ❻
Out[26]: array([[ 0,  1,  2,  3,  4],
                [-2, -1,  0,  1,  2],
                [-4, -3, -2, -1,  0],
                [-6, -5, -4, -3, -2],
                [-8, -7, -6, -5, -4]])
```

❶ Creates an ndarray object for the number of upward movements from 0 to m.

❷ Calculating the squares by a vectorized operation.

❸ Calculating the powers of 2 by using the u object as a vector exponent.

❹ Resizes the u object from one dimension to two dimensions. The number of upward movements is now stored in each row.

❺ Transposes the u object to get a two-dimensional ndarray object d with the number of downward movements in each column.

❻ Combines the u and d objects to arrive at the net number of upward and downward movements. For instance, +2 means "two more upward movements than downward movements" or -1 means "one more downward movement than upward movements."[2]

Equipped with a matrix containing the net number of movements in the binomial tree, simulation of the stock price process boils down to a single line of code:

```
In [27]: S = S0 * np.exp(sigma * math.sqrt(dt) * (u - 2 * d))  ❶
         S  ❷
Out[27]: array([[ 36.000,  39.786,  43.970,  48.595,  53.706],
                [ 29.474,  32.574,  36.000,  39.786,  43.970],
                [ 24.132,  26.669,  29.474,  32.574,  36.000],
```

---

2 Note that only the numbers on and above the diagonal are relevant. Numbers below the diagonal can be ignored. They result from the specific vectorized operations implemented on the ndarray object.

```
                  [ 19.757,  21.835,  24.132,  26.669,  29.474],
                  [ 16.176,  17.877,  19.757,  21.835,  24.132]])
```

❶ The vectorized simulation of the stock price process (binomial tree).

❷ Only the numbers on and above the diagonal are relevant.

The valuation of both the European and American put options is also vectorized to
some extent. A single loop over the time steps remains:

```
In [28]: h = np.maximum(K - S, 0)  ❶
         h  ❷
Out[28]: array([[  4.000,   0.214,   0.000,   0.000,   0.000],
                [ 10.526,   7.426,   4.000,   0.214,   0.000],
                [ 15.868,  13.331,  10.526,   7.426,   4.000],
                [ 20.243,  18.165,  15.868,  13.331,  10.526],
                [ 23.824,  22.123,  20.243,  18.165,  15.868]])

In [29]: V = h.copy()  ❸

In [30]: # European option pricing
         for t in range(m - 1, -1, -1):  ❹
             V[0:-1, t] = df * (q * V[:-1, t + 1] +
                          (1-q) * V[1:, t + 1])  ❹

In [31]: V[0, 0]  ❺
Out[31]: 3.977145694118792

In [32]: # American option pricing
         for t in range(m - 1, -1, -1):  ❻
             V[0:-1, t] = df * (q * V[:-1, t + 1] +
                          (1-q) * V[1:, t + 1])  ❻
             V[:, t] = np.maximum(h[:, t], V[:, t])  ❻

In [33]: V
Out[33]: array([[  4.540,   2.307,   0.784,   0.000,   0.000],
                [ 10.526,   7.426,   4.249,   1.771,   0.000],
                [ 15.868,  13.331,  10.526,   7.426,   4.000],
                [ 20.243,  18.165,  15.868,  13.331,  10.526],
                [ 23.824,  22.123,  20.243,  18.165,  15.868]])

In [34]: V[0, 0]  ❼
Out[34]: 4.5395605952243
```

❶ The calculation of the inner value of the put option, fully vectorized this time.

❷ As before, only the numbers on and above the diagonal are relevant.

❸ Creates a copy of the h object.

❹ The partly vectorized valuation algorithm for the European put option.

❺ The present value of the European put option.

❻ The partly vectorized valuation algorithm for the American put option.

❼ The present value of the American put option.

European and American Options

The beauty of the (recombining) binomial option pricing model of Cox, Ross, and Rubinstein (1979) not only lies in its simplicity but also in the fact that it can be used to value both European options and American options with high accuracy in an efficient manner. In the limit, making time steps infinitely small, the model converges to the Black-Scholes-Merton (1973) model, which is another advantage.

Speed Comparison

Vectorizing code not only makes Python code more concise, but it generally allows for significant speed improvements. The following code snippets implement the previous algorithms for a speed comparison based on a larger, more realistic number of time steps. First, the basic numerical parameters need to be adjusted:

```
In [35]: m = 500   ❶
         dt = T / m
         df = math.exp(-r * dt)
         up = math.exp(sigma * math.sqrt(dt))
         down = 1 / up
         q = (1 / df - down) / (up - down)
         q
Out[35]: 0.5044724639230862
```

❶ Increases the number of time intervals to a realistic level, yielding rather accurate numerical option values.

The function `binomial_looping()` integrates all elements of the *loop-based implementation* of the simulation and valuation algorithm for the American put option:

```
In [36]: def binomial_looping():
             # stock price simulation in binomial tree
             S = np.zeros((m + 1, m + 1))
             S[0, 0] = S0
             z = 1
             for t in range(1, m + 1):
                 for i in range(0, z):
                     S[i, t] = S[i, t - 1] * up
                     S[i + 1 ,t] = S[i, t - 1] * down
                 z += 1
             # inner value calculation
```

```
        h = np.zeros_like(S)
        z = 1
        for t in range(0, m + 1):
            for i in range(0, z):
                h[i, t] = max(K - S[i, t], 0)
            z += 1
        # American option pricing
        V = np.zeros_like(S)
        V[:, -1] = h[:, -1]
        z = 0
        for t in range(m - 1, -1, -1):
            for i in range(0, m - z):
                V[i, t] = df * (q * V[i, t + 1] +
                                (1 - q) * V[i + 1, t + 1])
                V[i, t] = max(h[i, t], V[i, t])
            z += 1
        return V[0, 0]
```

The execution takes less than 200 milliseconds on the author's computer:

```
In [37]: %time binomial_looping()
         CPU times: user 190 ms, sys: 4.69 ms, total: 194 ms
         Wall time: 190 ms

Out[37]: 4.486374777505983

In [38]: %timeit binomial_looping()
         173 ms ± 2.48 ms per loop (mean ± std. dev. of 7 runs, 10 loops each)
```

The function `binomial_vectorization()` integrates all elements of the *vectorized implementation* of the simulation and valuation algorithm for the American put option:

```
In [39]: def binomial_vectorization():
             u = np.arange(m + 1)
             u = np.resize(u, (m + 1, m + 1))
             d = u.T
             # stock price simulation
             S = S0 * np.exp(sigma * math.sqrt(dt) * (u - 2 * d))
             # inner value calculation
             h = np.maximum(K - S, 0)
             # American option pricing
             V = h.copy()
             for t in range(m-1, -1, -1):
                 V[0:-1, t] = df * (q * V[:-1, t + 1] +
                                    (1-q) * V[1:, t + 1])
                 V[:, t] = np.maximum(h[:, t], V[:, t])
             return V[0, 0]
```

This implementation is about 40 times faster than the loop-based one, which impressively illustrates the power of vectorized implementation approaches in terms of performance improvements:

```
In [40]: %time binomial_vectorization()
         CPU times: user 4.67 ms, sys: 2.39 ms, total: 7.07 ms
         Wall time: 8.73 ms

Out[40]: 4.486374777506075

In [41]: %timeit binomial_vectorization()
         4.7 ms ± 252 µs per loop (mean ± std. dev. of 7 runs, 100 loops each)
```

Infrastructure and Performance

All absolute times reported here are dependent both on the hardware and software configuration used. For instance, you can use NumPy in combination with the Math Kernel Library (MKL) from Intel (*https://oreil.ly/dWyk9*). This combination can significantly speed up numerical operations on Intel processor-based systems. Relative times and speed-up factors should be roughly similar on different infrastructures.

Black-Scholes-Merton Option Pricing

A static simulation version of the Black-Scholes-Merton (1973) model for option pricing is discussed in Chapter 5. This section introduces a *dynamic simulation version* for their seminal option pricing model. For additional background information on the model, refer to Chapter 5.

The stochastic differential equation for the Black-Scholes-Merton (1973) economy is given by

$$dS_t = rS_t dt + \sigma S_t dZ_t$$

where $S_t \in \mathbb{R}_{>0}$ is the stock price at time t, $r \in \mathbb{R}_{\geq 0}$ is the constant short rate, $\sigma \in \mathbb{R}_{>0}$ is the constant volatility factor, and Z_t is an arithmetic Brownian motion (see Glasserman (2004, chapter 3) and Hilpisch (2018, chapter 12)).

Monte Carlo Simulation of Stock Price Paths

Assume a finite set of relevant points in time $\mathcal{T} \equiv \{t_0 = 0, t_1, t_2, \ldots, t_M = T\}$, with $M + 1, M > 1$, and a fixed interval length of Δt. The stock price $S_t, 0 < t \leq T$, given the previous stock price $S_{t - \Delta t}$, can then be simulated according to the difference equation

$$S_t = S_{t - \Delta t} \cdot \exp\left(\left(r - \frac{\sigma^2}{2}\right)\Delta t + \sigma\sqrt{\Delta t}z\right)$$

where z is a standard normally distributed random variable. This scheme is called *Euler discretization*. It is known to be accurate in that it ensures convergence of the discrete time process to the continuous time process for Δt converging to 0.

The dynamic Monte Carlo simulation is—with the background knowledge from the static simulation in Chapter 5—straightforward to implement in Python. Figure 6-1 shows 10 simulated stock price paths:

```
In [43]: S0 = 36.   ❶
         K = 40.    ❶
         r = 0.06   ❶
         T = 1.0    ❶
         sigma = 0.2  ❶

In [44]: M = 100    ❷
         I = 50000  ❷

In [45]: dt = T / M  ❷
         dt  ❷
Out[45]: 0.01

In [46]: df = math.exp(-r * dt)   ❷
         df  ❷
Out[46]: 0.9994001799640054

In [47]: from numpy.random import default_rng
         rng = default_rng(100)

In [48]: rn = rng.standard_normal((M + 1, I))   ❸
         rn  ❸
Out[48]: array([[ -1.160,   0.290,   0.780, ...,   1.890,   0.050,  -0.760],
                [  0.460,  -1.400,   0.140, ...,  -1.350,   0.150,  -0.530],
                [  0.200,  -0.040,  -0.730, ...,   2.140,   0.170,  -0.340],
                ...,
                [ -0.220,  -1.310,   0.730, ...,  -0.820,  -0.600,  -0.400],
                [ -2.130,  -1.240,   0.580, ...,   0.960,   0.890,   0.780],
                [  2.130,  -0.410,   0.710, ...,   1.190,   0.100,  -0.520]])

In [49]: S = np.zeros_like(rn)   ❹
         S[0] = S0   ❹
         S  ❹
Out[49]: array([[ 36.000,  36.000,  36.000, ...,  36.000,  36.000,  36.000],
                [  0.000,   0.000,   0.000, ...,   0.000,   0.000,   0.000],
                [  0.000,   0.000,   0.000, ...,   0.000,   0.000,   0.000],
                ...,
                [  0.000,   0.000,   0.000, ...,   0.000,   0.000,   0.000],
                [  0.000,   0.000,   0.000, ...,   0.000,   0.000,   0.000],
                [  0.000,   0.000,   0.000, ...,   0.000,   0.000,   0.000]])

In [50]: for t in range(1, M + 1):
             S[t] = S[t - 1] * np.exp((r - sigma ** 2 / 2) * dt +
```

```
                              sigma * math.sqrt(dt) * rn[t])  ❺

In [51]: S  ❺
Out[51]: array([[ 36.000,   36.000,   36.000,  ...,   36.000,   36.000,   36.000],
                [ 36.349,   35.023,   36.114,  ...,   35.056,   36.119,   35.633],
                [ 36.508,   35.009,   35.602,  ...,   36.601,   36.259,   35.402],
                ...,
                [ 42.689,   39.760,   40.681,  ...,   37.516,   47.893,   42.846],
                [ 40.921,   38.804,   41.175,  ...,   38.260,   48.769,   43.534],
                [ 42.716,   38.499,   41.782,  ...,   39.200,   48.884,   43.103]])

In [52]: from pylab import mpl, plt
         plt.style.use('seaborn')
         mpl.rcParams['font.family'] = 'serif'
         mpl.rcParams['savefig.dpi'] = 300

In [53]: plt.figure(figsize=(10, 6))
         plt.plot(S[:, :10]);   ❻
```

❶ The financial parameters are as before.

❷ These are the Monte Carlo simulation parameters (paths, time steps, length of time interval, discount factor for single time interval).

❸ A two-dimensional ndarray object with standard normally distributed random numbers of appropriate size is generated.

❹ Another two-dimensional ndarray object of the same shape is instantiated, and the initial values for the single stock price paths are set.

❺ The single stock price paths are simulated based on the initial stock prices, the random number matrix, and the difference equation for the geometric Brownian motion.

❻ Plots the first 10 simulated paths.

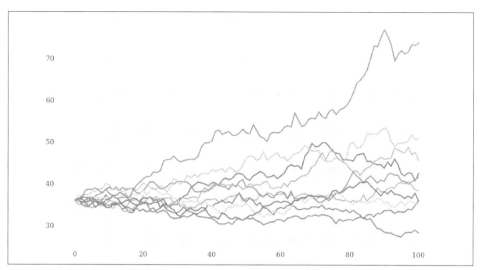

Figure 6-1. Simulated stock price paths for Black-Scholes-Merton (1973)

As in the static case, the end-of-period values of the stock price can be visualized in the form of a histogram (see Figure 6-2):

```
In [54]: ST = S[-1]
         plt.figure(figsize=(10, 6))
         plt.hist(ST, bins=35, color='b', label='frequency');
         plt.axvline(ST.mean(), color='r', label='mean')
         plt.axvline(ST.mean() + ST.std(), ls='--', color='y', label='sd up')
         plt.axvline(ST.mean() - ST.std(), ls='-.', color='y', label='sd down')
         plt.legend(loc=0);
In [55]: S0 * math.exp(r * T)   ❶
Out[55]: 38.22611567563295

In [56]: ST.mean()   ❷
Out[56]: 38.25248936738523
```

❶ Mathematically expected value for S_T.

❷ The average over all simulated values ST.

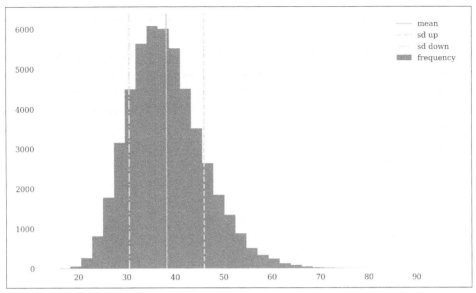

Figure 6-2. Frequency distribution of simulated end-of-period stock prices for Black-Scholes-Merton (1973)

Monte Carlo Valuation of the European Put Option

The Monte Carlo estimator for the price of the European put option is

$$P_0 = e^{-rT} \frac{1}{I} \sum_{i=1}^{I} \max\left(K - S_T(i), 0\right)$$

where I is the number of simulated price paths. Against this background, European put option pricing boils down to a few lines of Python code only given the simulated stock price paths. Figure 6-3 shows a histogram of the simulated inner values at maturity:

```
In [57]: h = np.maximum(K - ST, 0)    ❶
         h    ❶
Out[57]: array([ 0.000,    1.501,    0.000, ...,    0.800,    0.000,    0.000])

In [58]: plt.figure(figsize=(10, 6))
         plt.hist(h, color='b', bins=35);    ❷
In [59]: math.exp(-r * T) * h.mean()    ❸
Out[59]: 3.818117261795047
```

❶ Calculates the inner values in vectorized fashion.

❷ Plots the frequency distribution of the inner values at maturity, illustrating the highly asymmetric payoff that is typical for an option.[3]

❸ Calculates the average over all inner values and discounts the average to the present.

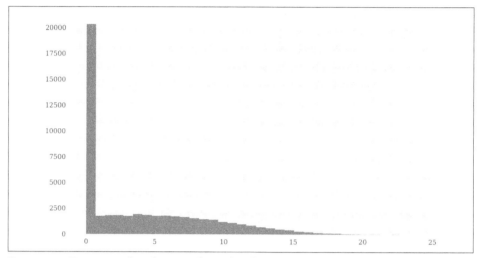

Figure 6-3. Frequency distribution of simulated inner values at maturity for the European put option

Monte Carlo Valuation of the American Put Option

The valuation of American (put) options based on Monte Carlo simulation is a bit more involved. The most popular algorithm in this regard is the *Least-Squares Monte Carlo* (LSM) algorithm from Longstaff and Schwartz (2001) because it is relatively simple and efficient to apply from a numerical and computational perspective. The scope of this chapter does not allow us to go into details. However, it allows us to present a concise, highly vectorized Python implementation. For an in-depth treatment of the LSM algorithm applied to the Black-Scholes-Merton (1973) model economy, including Python code, refer to Hilpisch (2015, chapter 7).

The following Python code implements the LSM algorithm for American option valuation:

---

3 Here, as also often seen in practice, there is a large number of cases for which the option expires worthless, that is, with a payoff of 0.

```
In [60]: h = np.maximum(K - S, 0)  ❶

In [61]: # Least-Squares Monte Carlo Valuation (LSM algorithm)
         V = h[-1]  ❷
         for t in range(M - 1, 0, -1):  ❸
             reg = np.polyfit(S[t], df * V, deg=5)  ❹
             C = np.polyval(reg, S[t])  ❹
             V = np.where(h[t] > C, h[t], df * V)  ❺

In [62]: df * V.mean()  ❻
Out[62]: 4.454837750511421
```

❶ Calculates the inner values over the complete stock price path ndarray object.

❷ Sets the initial simulated American option price values to the inner values at maturity.

❸ The algorithm also works based on backward induction, starting at $T - \Delta t$ and stopping at Δt.

❹ This is the central step of the algorithm during which the continuation values are estimated (approximated) based on the OLS regression of the present simulated option values against the stock price levels.

❺ If the inner value is higher than the estimated (approximated) continuation value, exercise takes place and otherwise not.

❻ The present value is calculated as the average over the American option price vector at $t = \Delta t$ as derived based on the LSM algorithm and discounted for the last remaining time interval to the present $t = 0$.

Early Exercise and Monte Carlo Simulation

The efficient, Monte Carlo simulation–based valuation of options and derivatives with early exercise features had been a mainly unsolved problem until the end of the 1990s. At the beginning of the 2000s only, researchers were able to propose computationally efficient algorithms to deal with early exercise in a simulation context. As often in science and finance, once such an algorithm is known—such as the LSM algorithm—the implementation and application almost seem quite natural. After all, only a few lines of Python code are needed to accurately value the American put option in this section based on simulation. Nevertheless, the LSM algorithm must be considered a major breakthrough that helped to kick off the computational period in finance (see Chapter 1).

Conclusions

This chapter presents in a rather informal manner two popular, dynamically complete financial models. The first is the so-called *recombining binomial tree model* by Cox-Ross-Rubinstein (1979). The beauty of it lies in its simplicity and that it allows one to implement European and American option pricing in a numerically efficient way and based on high school mathematics only. It is also a good "teaching and understanding" tool as compared to continuous time financial models that require advanced stochastic calculus.

The second model is a *dynamic Monte Carlo simulation version* of the Black-Scholes-Merton (1973) continuous time option pricing model. Using NumPy simulation techniques, dynamic Monte Carlo simulation can also be implemented in a numerically efficient manner. Even the computationally demanding Least-Squares Monte Carlo algorithm by Longstaff and Schwartz (2001), involving a time-consuming OLS regression step, is quite fast when implemented based on vectorization techniques.

In summary, NumPy, with its powerful vectorization capabilities, has proven once again that it allows not only for concise algorithmic code but also for fast execution times—even in the context of more realistic and complex dynamic model economies.

Further Resources

Papers cited in this chapter:

Black, Fischer and Myron Scholes. 1973. "The Pricing of Options and Corporate Liabilities." *Journal of Political Economy* 81 (3): 638–659.

Cox, John, Stephen Ross and Mark Rubinstein. 1979. "Option Pricing: A Simplified Approach." *Journal of Financial Economics* 7 (3): 229–263.

Duffie, Darrell. 1986. "Stochastic Equilibria: Existence, Spanning Number, and the *No Expected Gains from Financial Trade* Hypothesis." *Econometrica* 54 (5): 1161–1183.

Longstaff, Francis and Eduardo Schwartz. 2001. "Valuing American Options by Simulation: A Simple Least Squares Approach." *Review of Financial Studies* 14 (1): 113–147.

Merton, Robert. 1973. "Theory of Rational Option Pricing." *Bell Journal of Economics and Management Science* (4): 141–183.

Books cited in this chapter:

Duffie, Darrell. 1988. *Security Markets—Stochastic Models*. San Diego: Academic Press.

Glasserman, Paul. 2004. *Monte Carlo Methods in Financial Engineering.* New York: Springer Verlag.

Hilpisch, Yves. 2018. *Python for Finance.* 2nd ed. Sebastopol: O'Reilly.

Hilpisch, Yves. 2015. *Derivatives Analytics with Python.* Wiley Finance.

Pliska, Stanley. 1997. *Introduction to Mathematical Finance.* Malden and Oxford: Blackwell Publishers.

## CHAPTER 7

Where to Go from Here?

An investment in knowledge pays the best interest.

> —Benjamin Franklin

Politics is for the present, but an equation is for eternity.

> —Albert Einstein

Congratulations. You have reached the final chapter of the book. If you have followed the chapters diligently, you have already encountered many important ideas and concepts in both financial theory and Python programming. That is great. The topics covered in this book, both with regard to breadth and depth, represent good starting points for exploring the exciting and fast-changing world of computational finance. However, there is much more to explore and learn. This final chapter provides suggestions for moving on and going deeper in one or several directions in Python for finance.

Mathematics

This book makes use of different mathematical tools and techniques, such as from linear algebra, probability theory, and optimization theory. The tools and techniques applied to financial problems are fairly standard and do not require advanced mathematical skills to be put to beneficial use with Python. However, modern finance can be considered an *applied mathematics discipline*, with some areas relying heavily on advanced mathematics—such as option pricing or financial risk management.

The following list provides references for several standard textbooks that can be used to improve your mathematical skills for finance:

Aleskerov, Fuad, Hasan Ersel and Dmitri Piontkovski. 2011. *Linear Algebra for Economists*. Heidelberg: Springer Verlag.

Bhattacharya, Rabi and Edward Waymire. 2007. *A Basic Course in Probability Theory*. New York: Springer Verlag.

Jacod, Jean and Philip Protter. 2004. *Probability Essentials*. Berlin and Heidelberg: Springer Verlag.

Pemberton, Malcolm and Nicholas Rau. 2016. *Mathematics for Economists—An Introductory Textbook*. 4th ed. Manchester and New York: Manchester University Press.

Protter, Philip. 2005. *Stochastic Integration and Differential Equations*. 2nd ed. Berlin and Heidelberg: Springer Verlag.

Rudin,Walter. 1987. *Real and Complex Analysis*. 3rd ed. London: McGraw-Hill.

Sundaram, Rangarajan. 1996. *A First Course in Optimization Theory*. Cambridge: Cambridge University Press.

Williams, David. 1991. *Probability with Martingales*. Reprint 2001. Cambridge: Cambridge University Press.

Financial Theory

Finance is a vast domain with many different specializations. This book covers some of the most important and popular financial models, such as the mean-variance portfolio theory, the Capital Asset Pricing Model, and the Black-Scholes-Merton option pricing model. More generally speaking, it covers simple and more realistic static model economies (with two points in time only) as well as dynamic model economies to allow for uncertainty to resolve gradually over time. There are whole areas in mathematical finance that are not covered, however, such as continuous time models for option pricing that require additional, more advanced mathematical tools. The book also does not discuss, for example, such important financial topics as the Efficient Market Hypothesis (EMH).

The following list provides several basic finance books that can be used to get a broader overview of topics in financial theory and their underpinnings in economics:

Copeland, Thomas, Fred Weston and Kuldepp Shastri. 2005. *Financial Theory and Corporate Policy*. 4th ed. Boston: Addison Wesley.

Eichberger, Jürgen and Ian Harper. 1997. *Financial Economics*. New York: Oxford University Press.

Markowitz, Harry. 1959. *Portfolio Selection—Efficient Diversification of Investments*. New York: John Wiley & Sons.

Milne, Frank. 1995. *Finance Theory and Asset Pricing*. New York: Oxford University Press.

Pliska, Stanley. 1997. *Introduction to Mathematical Finance*. Malden and Oxford: Blackwell Publishers.

Rubinstein, Mark. 2006. *A History of the Theory of Investments*. Hoboken: Wiley Finance.

Varian, Hal. 1992. *Microeconomic Analysis*. 3rd ed. New York and London: W.W. Norton & Company.

For those who want to dig deeper into advanced mathematical modeling in finance, the following is a list of advanced textbooks about mathematical finance:

Baxter, Martin and Andrew Rennie. 1996. *Financial Calculus—An Introduction to Derivative Pricing*. Cambridge: Cambridge University Press.

Björk, Tomas. 2004. *Arbitrage Theory in Continuous Time*. 2nd ed. Oxford: Oxford University Press.

Delbaen, Freddy and Walter Schachermayer. 2006. *The Mathematics of Arbitrage*. Berlin: Springer Verlag.

Duffie, Darrell. 1988. *Security Markets—Stochastic Models*. San Diego: Academic Press.

Duffie, Darrell. 2001. *Dynamic Asset Pricing Theory*. 3rd ed. Princeton: Princeton University Press.

Elliot, Robert and Ekkehard Kopp. 2005. *Mathematics of Financial Markets*. 2nd ed. New York: Springer Verlag.

Glasserman, Paul. 2004. *Monte Carlo Methods in Financial Engineering*. New York: Springer Verlag.

Without doubt, it is also often rewarding and illuminating to read the seminal finance articles from which the financial models and theories originated. You will also find that many of these articles are surprisingly accessible. The following list references such articles, the selection of which is inspired by the topics and methods covered in this book:

Black, Fischer and Myron Scholes. 1973. "The Pricing of Options and Corporate Liabilities." *Journal of Political Economy* 81 (3): 638–659.

Boyle, Phelim. 1977. "Options: A Monte Carlo Approach." *Journal of Financial Economics* 4 (4): 322–338.

Cox, John and Stephen Ross. 1976. "The Valuation of Options for Alternative Stochastic Processes." *Journal of Financial Economics* (3): 145–166.

Cox, John, Jonathan Ingersoll and Stephen Ross. 1985. "A Theory of the Term Structure of Interest Rates." *Econometrica* 53 (2): 385–407.

Cox, John, Stephen Ross and Mark Rubinstein. 1979. "Option Pricing: A Simplified Approach." *Journal of Financial Economics* 7 (3): 229–263.

Duffie, Darrell. 1986. "Stochastic Equilibria: Existence, Spanning Number, and the *No Expected Gains from Financial Trade* Hypothesis." *Econometrica* 54 (5): 1161–1183.

Harrison, Michael and David Kreps. 1979. "Martingales and Arbitrage in Multiperiod Securities Markets." *Journal of Economic Theory* (20): 381–408.

Harrison, Michael and Stanley Pliska. 1981. "Martingales and Stochastic Integrals in the Theory of Continuous Trading." *Stochastic Processes and their Applications* (11): 215–260.

Heston, Steven. 1993. "A Closed-Form Solution for Options with Stochastic Volatility with Applications to Bond and Currency Options." *The Review of Financial Studies* 6 (2): 327–343.

Longstaff, Francis and Eduardo Schwartz. 2001. "Valuing American Options by Simulation: A Simple Least Squares Approach." *Review of Financial Studies* 14 (1): 113–147.

Markowitz, Harry. 1952. "Portfolio Selection." *Journal of Finance* 7 (1): 77–91.

Merton, Robert. 1976. "Option Pricing when the Underlying Stock Returns are Discontinuous." *Journal of Financial Economics*, 3 (3): 125–144.

Perold, André. 2004. "The Capital Asset Pricing Model." *Journal of Economic Perspectives* 18 (3): 3–24

Protter, Philip. 2001. "A Partial Introduction to Financial Asset Pricing Theory." *Stochastic Processes and their Applications* (91): 169–203.

Sharpe, William. 1964. "Capital Asset Prices: A Theory of Market Equilibrium under Conditions of Risk." *The Journal of Finance* 19 (3): 425–442.

For those looking for a single, comprehensive reference, the Market Risk Analysis book collection might be worth having a closer look:

Alexander, Carol. 2008. *Market Risk Analysis I—Quantitative Methods in Finance*. Chicester: John Wiley & Sons.

Alexander, Carol. 2008. *Market Risk Analysis II—Practical Financial Econometrics*. Chicester: John Wiley & Sons.

Alexander, Carol. 2008. *Market Risk Analysis III—Pricing, Hedging and Trading Financial Instruments*. Chicester: John Wiley & Sons.

Alexander, Carol. 2008. *Market Risk Analysis IV—Value-at-Risk Models*. Chicester: John Wiley & Sons.

Python Programming

Nowadays, there is a large number of resources available to learn Python programming. The following books have proven to be useful for me. When it comes to getting a better Python programmer in general and you want to pick only one from the list, you should go with the book by Ramalho (2021), which dives deep into the Python programming language itself:

Harrison, Matt. 2017. *Illustrated Guide to Python 3: A Complete Walkthrough of Beginning Python with Unique Illustrations Showing how Python Really Works*. http://hairysun.com.

McKinney, Wes. 2017. *Python for Data Analysis*. 2nd ed. Sebastopol: O'Reilly.

Ramalho, Luciano. 2021. *Fluent Python*. 2nd ed. Sebastopol: O'Reilly.

Ravenscroft, Anna, Steve Holden, and Alex Martelli. 2017. *Python in a Nutshell*. 3rd ed. Sebastopol: O'Reilly.

VanderPlas, Jake. 2016. *Python Data Science Handbook*. Sebastopol: O'Reilly.

Python for Finance

This book is my sixth book about Python applied to finance. You might wonder: "Why does the most basic, introductory textbook come only after the five other, more advanced textbooks?" There is probably not a short, simple answer. However, the writing of this book, *Financial Theory with Python*, was motivated by requests from my readers of the other books and from our online training program participants. Many were looking for a gentle introduction to both finance *and* Python programming—complementing the other books.[1] Therefore, *Financial Theory with Python* introduces both topics from scratch and thereby closes the initial gap, say, to get started with the book *Python for Finance*, for which the reader is expected to have some background in both finance and programming.

---

[1] I like to think of this book as being what *The Hobbit* by J. R. R. Tolkien is to his *Lord of the Rings* trilogy. Of course, there is no literary comparison implied here.

My other five books are:

Hilpisch, Yves. 2020. *Artificial Intelligence in Finance: A Python-Based Guide*. Sebastopol: O'Reilly.

Hilpisch, Yves. 2020. *Python for Algorithmic Trading: From Idea to Cloud Deployment*. Sebastopol: O'Reilly.

Hilpisch, Yves. 2018. *Python for Finance: Mastering Data-Driven Finance*. 2nd ed. Sebastopol: O'Reilly.

Hilpisch, Yves. 2017. *Listed Volatility and Variance Derivatives: A Python-Based Guide*. Wiley Finance.

Hilpisch, Yves. 2015. *Derivatives Analytics with Python: Data Analysis, Models, Simulation, Calibration and Hedging*. Wiley Finance.

Financial Data Science

Data science has become an important discipline and function in basically every industry. In the same way, *Financial Data Science* has developed to become a core discipline and function in finance. Ever-increasing data volumes make the application of more advanced and sophisticated data logistics and management approaches necessary. Excel spreadsheets are for sure not enough anymore. My book *Python for Finance* is primarily about Python for financial data science. Relevant topics that are covered in parts II and III of that book include: data types and structures, numerical computing with NumPy, data analysis with pandas, object-oriented programming, data visualization, financial time series, input/output operations, performance Python, mathematical tools, stochastics, and statistics (including basic machine learning). After you have finished *Financial Theory with Python*, the book *Python for Finance* represents a natural next step in leveling up your Python for finance skills.

Algorithmic Trading

Systematic or algorithmic trading has become the standard not only for hedge funds but even for many retail traders. The availability of powerful APIs, even to retail traders with smaller budgets, has given rise to a proliferation of algorithmic trading strategies practically across all asset classes. While larger financial institutions in general have dedicated teams for every step of the trading process—from data analysis, research, and backtesting to deployment, monitoring, and risk management—retail traders generally need to take care of all of this on their own.

What a few years back might have seemed an almost impossible endeavor for a single person can nowadays be relatively easily accomplished due to the powerful ecosystem of Python. Retail traders with Python programming skills can in principle set up an algorithmic trading operation within weeks or even days. My book *Python for*

Algorithmic Trading covers the main Python skills required in this context and leads the reader from data management and idea generation to the backtesting of strategies and their automated deployment in the cloud.

Part IV of *Python for Finance* also covers key skills in Python for algorithmic trading. While it's not as detailed as *Python for Algorithmic Trading*, readers should nevertheless be able, based on the self-contained resources in *Python for Finance*, to efficiently generate and deploy a trading strategy that places trades automatically.

For both the *Python for Algorithmic Trading* book and part IV of *Python for Finance*, it is helpful but not necessarily required for the reader to have studied *Financial Theory with Python* and *Python for Finance* (Parts I, II, and III) beforehand.

Computational Finance

Quantitative and computational finance have long been dominated by compiled programming languages, such as C or C++. This is because the speed of the execution of oftentimes complex numerical computations and simulations is of the essence—in particular when scalability is required by larger financial institutions. While pure Python might indeed be too slow to implement, say, computationally demanding simulation algorithms, packages such as NumPy and pandas allow much faster execution times when used appropriately. Such packages provide high-level programming APIs to functionality that is implemented in performant C code in general. This often allows for speed-ups compared to pure Python code of 10–30 times, making Python plus specialized packages a valid alternative for computational finance these days.

My book *Derivatives Analytics with Python* introduces the major mathematical and financial concepts required to price and hedge derivatives in a market-based way—that is, based on market-calibrated pricing models. The book provides a self-contained Python code base that implements all algorithms and techniques from scratch, making heavy use of the capabilities of NumPy. Those having read *Financial Theory with Python* and *Python for Finance* (parts I, II, and III) are well equipped to deepen their knowledge in mathematical and computational finance with *Derivatives Analytics with Python*.

Part V of *Python for Finance* develops a simple version of my derivatives pricing library DX Analytics (*https://dx-analytics.com*). It shows how the concepts, approaches, and numerical methods from *Derivatives Analytics with Python* can be used to create a flexible and powerful pricing library based on Monte Carlo simulation. Those who need additional models and even more capabilities—such as for risk measurement and management—can, of course, use the DX Analytics open source package itself.

Volatility as an asset class has become quite important over recent years. Be it to manage risk or to generate additional alpha, listed volatility and variance derivatives are used around the globe in systematic fashion. The book *Listed Volatility and Variance Derivatives* introduces the main concepts of trading and pricing such financial instruments and provides a self-contained Python code base illustrating all concepts—such as the model-free replication of variance or the calculation volatility indices—in an easy-to-reproduce way.

Artificial Intelligence

It is safe to assume that artificial intelligence (AI) will play a dominant role in finance in the future, as it does already in so many other industries. Basically every financial institution has initiated projects to explore the potential of AI to improve operations, to save costs, to generate alpha, and so forth. Algorithms from machine learning, deep learning, and reinforcement learning are basically tested and in use in every field of finance. Researchers and academics are also publishing papers at the intersection of AI and finance with ever-increasing speeds.

My book *Artificial Intelligence in Finance* provides in part I background and historical information about AI and its success stories. It proceeds in part II to discuss traditional financial theory and recent advances in the field, such as data-driven finance and AI-first finance. Part II also discusses machine learning as a process. Part III of the book introduces and discusses major models and algorithms from deep learning, such as dense neural networks (DNNs), recurrent neural networks (RNNs), and reinforcement learning (Q-learning). Part IV of the book illustrates how statistical inefficiencies in financial markets can be economically exploited through algorithmic trading, that is, by a trading bot who interactively learns how to trade based on a Q-learning algorithm. Part V of the book discusses consequences of AI-first finance for the competitive landscape in the financial industry. It also discusses the possibility of a financial singularity—that is, a point in time from which an artificial financial intelligence (AFI) exists that, for example, can generate (almost) perfect predictions about future prices in the markets.

The book *Artificial Intelligence in Finance* can be considered complementary to the book *Python for Algorithmic Trading* in that it discusses in detail the formulation, backtesting, and risk management of AI-powered algorithmic trading strategies. Readers do not have to have read the algorithmic trading book before diving into the fascinating world of AI in finance. However, a solid understanding of Python for finance, based on this book and parts I to III of *Python for Finance*, is helpful.

Other Resources

You might have noticed that this section discusses only my own books about Python for finance. The very purpose of this section is to guide the reader who has finished this book through my other works. For sure, there are many other resources in book form available today that cover, for example, Python topics related to finance or machine learning algorithms as applied to finance. While other authors also offer valuable content and guidance, readers who like this book will probably also like my other books since they are similar in style and approach.

While some readers learn most efficiently using books and the accompanying code only, others like a more interactive, guided learning experience. My company The Python Quants GmbH has for years offered comprehensive online training programs that teach the skills from my books and much more in a systematic, structured way. There are three different online training programs available at the time of this writing:

- Python for Algorithmic Trading (*https://oreil.ly/r4l7y*)
- Python for Computational Finance (*https://oreil.ly/0h4Ej*)
- Python for Asset Management (*https://oreil.ly/ubbLm*)

These three programs can also be combined into a single program for those who benefit from all core topics (*https://oreil.ly/xc4qe*).

Final Words

Congratulations again. With *Financial Theory with Python* you have laid the foundations for your next exciting steps with Python for finance. This chapter provides a wealth of resources for you to explore. If you see Python for finance as a skill that you train for regularly, diligently, and systematically, you will probably reach black-belt level sometime soon. Such an achievement is not only personally rewarding, it also guarantees you a successful future because Python for finance has undoubtedly become a key skill in the financial industry. May the Python force be with you.

Index

ndarray, 7, 27
    dot product, 31
    for linear algebra and probability theory, 34
    loops, 151-154
    matrices, 39
    probability measure, 30
net present value, 25
np.linalg.lstsq function, 71-72, 137-138
np.linalg.solve function, 137
numeraire, 20
NumPy, 8
    dot product, 31
    financial asset modeling, 28
    installing, 12
    least-squares approach, 137-138
    for linear algebra and probability theory, 34
    loops, 151-154
    matrices, 39
    OLS (ordinary least-squares) regression,
        71-72
    vector modeling, 7, 27-28, 154-157

O

OLS (ordinary least-squares) regression, 71-72
opening Jupyter Notebooks, 13-15
opportunity costs, 24
optimal portfolio choice, 83
    constrained optimization problem, 94
    expected utility and, 95-98
    unconstrained optimization problem, 95
ordered pairs, 21
ordinary least-squares (OLS) regression, 71-72
outflows (cash), 21

P

pandas, 8, 12
paying interest, 23
payoff of call options, 35-36
    European, 6
    replication, 37-40
Pliska, Stanley, 59, 147
portfolio strategy, 39
power set, 60
present value, 24-25
price process of financial assets, 28
pricing by expectation, 51
probability measure, 29, 119
probability space, 29, 60, 119
probability theory

    contingent claims in, 35
    in discrete finance models, 122
    NumPy and ndarray for, 34
probability, defined, 119
programming language of finance, 5
pure investment problem, 93
Python
    finance and, 4, 5
    installing, 10-15
    Quant Platform, 9
    requirements for, 8-9
    resources for information, 173-177
Python environment, creating, 11
Python loops, 151-154, 157-159

Q

Quant Platform, 9

R

random variables
    contingent claims as, 35
    payoffs represented by, 6
    in static economy, 119
rate of return
    defined, 23
    expected, 32
real assets, 18
real numbers, 6, 20
recombining binomial tree, 149
relative price, 100, 104, 112
replication, 37-40
    approximate, 71-72
    of contingent claims, 124-125
    dual problem, 130
    super-replication, 67-70
representative agents
    complete market equilibrium pricing,
        99-106
    defined, 83
    incomplete market equilibrium pricing,
        106-115
    static economy pricing, 143-144
requirements for Python, 8-9
resources for information
    AI (artificial intelligence), 176
    algorithmic trading, 174
    computational finance, 175
    data science, 174
    financial theory, 170-173

mathematics, 169-170
  Python, 173-177
return
  defined, 23
  expected, 32-33
risk, 29-34
  ambiguity versus, 30
  expectation, 31-32
  expected return, 32-33
  hedging, 67
  probability measure, 29
  volatility, 33-34
risk-adjusted discount factors, 80
risk-less interest rates, 102
risk-neutral pricing, 67
risk-return trade-off in market equilibrium, 79

S

scalar addition/multiplication, 26
SciPy, 9
  installing, 12
  minimization problems, 69-70
  minimize function, 96
Second Fundamental Theorem of Asset Pricing,
  52, 132
security market line (SML), 77
set of attainable contingent claims, 42, 61
Sharpe, William, 59
short selling, 38
simple arbitrage, 50
SML (security market line), 77
span
  defined, 42, 61
  of market payoff matrix, 125
  matplotlib and, 43-47
standard basis for vector space, 48
state prices, 102
state space, 29, 60
states of economy, 26
static economy, 19, 117
  Black-Scholes-Merton option pricing,
    133-138
  contingent claims, 124-125
  financial assets, 122-124
  Fundamental Theorems of Asset Pricing,
    129-133
  market completeness, 125-129
  Merton jump-diffusion option pricing,
    138-143

representative agent pricing, 143-144
  uncertainty, 118-121
static three-state economy (see three-state
  model economy)
strike price, 35
super-replication, 67-70
SymPy, 9
  installing, 12
  martingale measures, 105
system of linear equations, 37

T

technology trends in finance, 3
three-state model economy, 59
  approximate replication, 71-72
  attainable contingent claims, 61-63
  CAPM (capital asset pricing model), 75-80
  CML (capital market line), 73-75
  financial assets, 60
  martingale pricing, 64-67
  risk-neutral pricing, 67
  super-replication, 67-70
  uncertainty, 60
time, 19
time-additive expected utility function, 98-99
time-additive utility functions, 90-93
trading strategy, 39
tuples in Python, 21-22
two-state model economy, 17
  agents, 18
  Arrow-Debreu securities, 47-49
  cash flow, 21-26
  contingent claims, 35-47
  financial assets, 28-29
  martingale pricing, 49-52
  money, 20
  MVP (mean-variance portfolio) theory,
    52-56
  real assets, 18
  risk, 29-34
  time, 19
  uncertainty, 26-28
two-tuples, 21

U

uncertainty, 5-8
  expected utility, 93-95
    optimal investment portfolio, 95-98
    time-additive, 98-99

About the Author

Dr. Yves J. Hilpisch is founder and CEO of The Python Quants (*http://tpq.io*), a group focusing on the use of open source technologies for financial data science, artificial intelligence, algorithmic trading, computational finance, and asset management. He is also founder and CEO of The AI Machine (*http://aimachine.io*), a company focused on AI-powered algorithmic trading via a proprietary strategy-execution platform.

In addition to this book, he is the author of the following books (*http://books.tpq.io*):

- *Artificial Intelligence in Finance* (O'Reilly, 2020)
- *Python for Algorithmic Trading* (O'Reilly, 2020)
- *Python for Finance* (2nd ed., O'Reilly, 2018)
- *Listed Volatility and Variance Derivatives* (Wiley, 2017)
- *Derivatives Analytics with Python* (Wiley, 2015)

Yves is an adjunct professor of Computational Finance and lectures on Algorithmic Trading at the CQF Program (*http://cqf.com*). He is also the director of the first online training programs leading to University Certificates in Python for Algorithmic Trading (*https://oreil.ly/Yyy1Y*), Python for Computational Finance (*https://oreil.ly/TirLm*), and Python for Asset Management (*https://oreil.ly/ubbLm*), respectively.

Yves wrote the financial analytics library *DX Analytics* (*http://dx-analytics.com*) and organizes meetups, conferences, and bootcamps about Python for quantitative finance and algorithmic trading in London, Frankfurt, Berlin, Paris, and New York. He has given keynote speeches at technology conferences in the United States, Europe, and Asia.

Colophon

The animal on the cover of *Financial Theory with Python* is a crowned moon snake (*Furina ornata*). More commonly known as the orange-naped snake, this small venemous snake is native to northern and northwestern Australia. It is commonly identified by the red blotch on its nape that is not completely enclosed by the black bands above and below it.

The crowned moon snake's conservation status is "Least Concern." Many of the animals on O'Reilly covers are endangered; all of them are important to the world.

The cover illustration is by Karen Montgomery, based on a black and white engraving from Lydekker's *Royal Natural History*. The cover fonts are Gilroy Semibold and Guardian Sans. The text font is Adobe Minion Pro; the heading font is Adobe Myriad Condensed; and the code font is Dalton Maag's Ubuntu Mono.

Lightning Source UK Ltd.
Milton Keynes UK
UKHW032022041121
393398UK00002B/7